THE
DANGER
WITHIN

MANUEL VASQUEZ

Pacific Press Publishing Association
Boise, Idaho
Oshawa, Ontario, Canada

Edited by B. Russell Holt
Designed by Dennis Ferree
Cover art by Lars Justinen
Typeset in 10/12 Century Schoolbook

Library of Congress Cataloging-in-Publication Data:
Vasquez, Manuel.
    The danger within : the New Age has already invaded your life
and home : do you know where it's lurking? / Manuel Vasquez.
        p.   cm.
    ISBN 0-8163-1152-8
    Includes bibliographical references.
    1. New Age movement—Controversial literature. 2. Occult-
ism—Religious aspects—Christianity. 3. United States—Religion—1960–   I. Title.
BP605.N48V37   1993
299'.93—dc20   92-44206
                                                    CIP

94 95 96 97 • 5 4

Dedication

To
Lori, Julie, and Sherri—
my three daughters, who are among
my greatest treasures in life.

Contents

Acknowledgments

This book could not have been written without the expertise and skillful assistance of the following people:

My wife, Nancy, for her untiring assistance in the research, the reading and rereading of the manuscript, and making editorial suggestions.

Evelyn Griffin, for her interest in this project and for the laborious task of typing the manuscript.

Will Baron, for his technical assistance regarding some of the concepts and terms expressed in this book.

And Bob Kyte, for challenging me to write this book.

Foreword

I'm angry! The devil is stealing some of God's most meaningful symbols and principles of life, combining them with Eastern pagan beliefs, and presenting this counterfeit version to the world as something new. New Age!

Take the rainbow, for example. Since I was a little child, my mother taught me, "The rainbow is God's sign to us that He will never again destroy the earth with a flood." Now the devil has stolen this symbol and made it the bridge from this world to his world. Every time I go into a toy store and see Rainbow Brite products, I have to cringe as I realize how subtle New Age beliefs have been woven into these toy characters. The pure, true meaning of God's rainbow has been tainted by the counterfeit.

The same thing is happening with Bible principles. The Bible says, "Nothing is impossible with God" (see Mark 10:27). With a seemingly minor alteration, we hear the New Age version: "Nothing is impossible." At first glance, it looks so close to the truth that it seems good. The problem is that it leaves out God. And therein lies the danger. Without God, this principle leads you 180 degrees from the real source of success.

One of the areas of great concern in New Age thinking is that of visualization. Visualizing is a wonderful God-given principle to help us achieve goals. But the danger is that the devil's New Age counterfeit of visualizing leads us to self-hypnosis and channeling, which are deadly!

Our children, especially, are being bombarded day in and day out with occult, New Age philosophy—from their breakfast cereal boxes and lunch pails to their entertainment and toys. Satan is doing a thorough job of indoctrinating and desensitizing them to the evils of spiritualism and the occult.

As you read this book, you will be able to sharpen your ability to detect and defend yourself and your family against this subtle New

Age influence that is infiltrating every facet of life. May God help you as you become more aware of the "danger within."

Kay Kuzma, Ed.D.
president, *Family Matters*

Preface

Speaking to many church groups and workers on the dangers of the New Age movement, I have been both alarmed at the general lack of knowledge of this movement and its tremendous influence, and gratified at the subsequent eye-opening experiences many have had.

The New Age movement is so diverse, subtle, and still evolving that it is difficult to define. However, most people, after getting a glimpse of what is behind this veil of deception, are able to begin putting together pieces of the New Age puzzle that heretofore have been seemingly unrelated. They begin to realize how they and their families have been (and are still being) personally affected by this new pagan influence.

We are fighting a war, a spiritual war, against supernatural forces. In order to win, we must first realize that we are in a war and then be able to identify the enemy. That is why I have written this book—to tear away the mask of the enemy, to expose his subtle tactics and demonic intentions, and then to offer Christians both a defensive armor and the ammunition for victory.

The names used in personal experiences throughout the book are fictitious in order to protect the privacy of those who have shared their experiences with me.

In the following chapters you will be able to take a close look at how the New Age influence has infiltrated music, medicine, entertainment, education, toys, and even Christian meditation.

It's time to stop playing with the enemy! For years many of us have been amusing ourselves to death with demon-inspired TV programs, movies, videos, and games. We have sought the forbidden fruit of astrology, mysticism, and privileged knowledge. Our eyes have been off the Saviour so long that our spiritual vision has become blurred and our discernment impaired. In our weakened spiritual condition, we have grabbed at the tempting morsels offered to us by the same hand that offered the glittering fruit to the innocent woman in the garden.

The New Age movement promotes the same lies presented so

long ago but in a candy coating to make them pleasing. But if we look closer, we will see that these "candied apples" are actually rotten to the core. Satan's New Age mask covers the horrible features of that same unscrupulous enemy whose insidious intent has long been first to ensnare and then to destroy.

Manuel Vasquez

CHAPTER

1

The New Age Has Already Touched Your Life

Whether you realize it or not, you have been touched by the New Age influence. Whether you can identify any of the New Age tenets or whether you have even heard of the "New Age movement," it has touched you. You may consider yourself an insulated, isolated, inoculated Christian, but you are not immune.

Without recognizing it as such, you may have New Age literature in your home—for example, Richard Bach's bestseller, *Jonathan Livingston Seagull,* or Dr. M. Scott Peck's *The Road Less Traveled.* You may have picked up on a New Age concept such as, "Whatever the mind can conceive, it can achieve." You may even be teaching such ideas to others. You may have sung the lyrics of "The Age of Aquarius" or "Déjà vu." You may have listened to New Age meditation music on the radio or perhaps even in your church. You may have tried meditation, visualizing, or listening to an "inner voice." You may have watched some of the New Age stars at the movies or on your television set. You may have purchased such products as New Age jewelry, rainbows, dragons, or pyramids. Out of curiosity, you may have read your horoscope in the daily newspaper. You may have visited a holistic health doctor or taken a karate or yoga class—not realizing you were being exposed to some of the powerful deceptions of the New Age movement.

Your children may be watching TV cartoons laced with sorcery and New Age themes, reading occult comics, or playing with their corresponding toys. They may even be caught up in the demonic Nintendo power-game mania. This is all part of the New Age scheme. Its tentacles are so widespread that it has infiltrated virtually every aspect of society.

The New Age movement has been called a conspiracy even by its advocates, who claim that "there are tens of thousands of entry points to this conspiracy. Wherever people share experiences, they connect sooner or later with each other and eventually with larger circles. Each day their number grows."[1]

Its conspirators, who number in the millions,[2] can be found teaching in the classroom, chairing executive corporate committees, supervising science laboratories, leading out in government, entertaining in the show biz world, and leading the way in the alternative medicine field. They are among the antiwar activists, the feminists, the pro-environmentalists; they are in health-related institutions and even in some Christian churches. They can be found among the white- as well as blue-collar workers and among every ethnic group. Some are self-declared, ardent proponents, while others quietly keep their New Age lifestyles at a low profile.

Marilyn Ferguson wrote *The Aquarian Conspiracy*, considered by some to be the "handbook" of the New Age movement. She affirms that

> the Aquarian Conspirators range across all levels of income and education, from the humblest to the highest. There are schoolteachers and office workers, famous scientists, government officials and lawmakers, artists and millionaires, taxi drivers and celebrities, leaders in medicine, education, law, psychology. Some are open in their advocacy, and their names may be familiar. Others are quiet about their involvement, believing they can be more effective if they are not identified with ideas that have all too often been misunderstood.[3]

One of these familiar New Age names is John Naisbitt, the prolific writer on corporate megatrends, who gave his testimony in the foreword for *The Aquarian Conspiracy*.

> Rarely has a book articulated and documented what so many of us were secretly thinking . . . my book, *Megatrends*, was the soft-core document on change; *The Aquarian Conspiracy* was "the hard-core stuff." . . . *Megatrends* spoke of

changes in our society; *The Aquarian Conspiracy* dealt with the change in ourselves, in our souls.[4]

The Christian Research Newsletter informed its readers that according to one researcher:

> Sociologists at U.C. Santa Barbara . . . estimate that as many as 12 million Americans could be considered active participants in the New Age Movement, and another 30 million are avidly interested. If all of these people were brought together in a church-like organization, it would be the third-largest religious denomination in America.[5]

In addition to the legions of sympathizers and open, self-declared New Age conspirators, tens of thousands more, including unsuspecting Christians, are caught up in its influence without even realizing it. These people are not consciously working in the New Age movement, but they have unknowingly bought into some phase of its philosophy.

Often I am asked to speak on the New Age. At the end of every presentation, people come up and speak with me. Some thank me profusely for making them aware of the New Age movement. Others express a genuine concern about some of the areas I have identified as New Age. Unsuspectingly, some of these folks, or a close friend of theirs, have become involved or have been practicing some aspect of the New Age. The New Age movement has quietly come in while we were asleep, like an odorless vapor that has enveloped the whole atmosphere, touching each of our lives, some more than others.

What is the New Age movement?

By now, you may be wondering, "Exactly what is this movement that has found such fertile ground and flourished so rapidly in America?" Twenty years ago—even a decade ago—few were aware of the widespread, evolving momentum the New Age movement was creating.

The New Age movement is an umbrella term used to describe a conglomeration or kaleidoscope of beliefs based on spiritualism, humanism, and Eastern mystical religions such as Hinduism, Buddhism, and Taoism. Johanna Michaelsen, in her book *Like*

Lambs to the Slaughter, says: "Western occultism and humanism have embraced Eastern mysticism to their bosom and the bizarre offspring of this union has been christened the New Age Movement."[6]

The New Age movement is a revival of such occult and spiritualistic practices as: reincarnation, mystical meditation, pantheism, oneness with the universe, channeling, numerology, astrology, parapsychology, holistic health of various types, and psychic phenomena. Thus the New Age is not really new, as Shirley MacLaine, one of the leading New Age proponents, admits:

> There's nothing new about the New Age. It is, as has been correctly reported, a compilation of many ancient spiritual points of view relating to belief, the nature of reality, the practice of living, ritual, and truth, all predominately originating in cultures other than those of the West.[7]

The New Age is a movement that seeks to cast off the claims of Christ on humanity and encourages human beings to look within, rather than outside of, themselves for spiritual growth and direction. The New Age movement is not easy to define, since it has no organized body, no written creed, and no apparent human leader. Instead, it is a powerful network of independent key individuals, small and large groups, whose common goal is a transformed America and a "new world order." It is a movement that is continually evolving and evading a definite description. Not every person in the New Age movement is knowingly participating in all of the hundreds of facets that make up this massive collusion. Most New Agers take those aspects that turn them on and leave the rest. In some cases, those following some aspect of New Age practice or espousing some New Age idea are not even aware that they are part of a massive movement, much less that certain other beliefs and practices are also a part of this alternative belief system. These people are not to be condemned or ostracized, but lovingly warned.

The New Age is so intriguing and diversified in its scope that it appeals to the very young and old alike. Three-year-olds are mesmerized by occult TV cartoons and Nintendo electronic games. Aging adults, who may have given up on conventional health treatments because they were dissatisfied with the results or received impersonal treatment, are experimenting with alternative holistic health and New Age pseudo-healers. Within the New Age movement, there is something for everyone—the housewife and the yuppie; the executive and the teenager; the senior citizen and the child.

One reason this movement is so alluring is that it gives a sense of self-control and power. It promises inner "spiritual" growth, discovery of one's "higher self," knowledge and understanding of the mystical world around us, personal insights for the future, and oneness with "God." There are no absolutes in New Age thinking. Whatever you decide is right, is right. Most of all, there is no biblical concept of sin, judgment, or death. There is only "karma," self-realization, and the cycles of life (reincarnation).

For example, in March 1989, Ozel Tendzin, spiritual leader of the Vajradhatu International Buddhists (the largest branch of Tibetan Buddhism in America), was exposed as having tested positive for the AIDS virus. The 3,500 members of Tendzin's group were stunned! Tendzin, whose homosexual activities were no secret, had been infected for several years, but did not acknowledge it until both male and female companions were found to be infected.

In a telephone interview, John Dart, *Los Angeles Times* religion editor, spoke with one of Tendzin's board members, Martin Janowitz, who stated, "We don't have a concept within our religion of moral or immoral sexual practices. We don't view, as do some other religions, homosexual relations as any kind of sin."[8]

What could be more appealing to human nature than to believe that there is no sin, that there is no death, that we can become as God, that we are gods—echoing the first New Age message by the old serpent in the tree six thousand years ago?

A paradigm shift

The "movers and shakers" of this New Age movement call it the Aquarian conspiracy to transform the world. The name *Aquarian* is derived from Aquarius, the eleventh astrological sign in the zodiac. Aquarius is the water bearer, pouring out refreshing, gently flowing water, symbolizing an age of peace, love, and spiritual enlightenment. Contrast this with the previous Age of Pisces, depicted by the symbol of two fish and called a "dark and violent" period of earth's history. Ironically, the Age of Pisces was the period in history when Christianity developed and spread throughout most of the world.

New Agers are working toward a paradigm shift that they claim is now taking place—a new way of thinking. A new mind-set. A new way of looking at the world, the universe, and life itself. Others describe it as a "quantum leap in consciousness," a sudden significant leap forward in global and universal awareness. New Agers compare this paradigm shift to other radical changes that have taken place in human experience—such as the enormous adjustments "flat earthers" had to make when Christopher Columbus proved the earth was round. This had a great impact on the sciences, literature, and education of that time. Textbooks had to be rewritten. Maps had to be revised to include the great expanse of the Pacific and the other half of the world.

Or this shift could be compared to the change that occurred around the turn of this century—a change that began as two brothers sat in church one Sunday morning listening intently as their preacher-father addressed one of the popular concerns of the day. "If God would have wanted men to fly," their father said, "He would have given us wings." Then and there, Orville and Wilbur Wright decided to prove their father wrong. And when they did, people around the world had to change their views on man's limitations and his ability, for the first time in history, to enter the domain of the birds. It was the beginning of the air age. The invention of the flying machine immensely modified the way people traveled, communicated, and fought wars. Technology and industry changed direction to accommodate the Wright brothers' invention.

In the same fashion, New Agers believe that the present paradigm shift involves extraordinary intervention from outer space, bombardment from the spirit world, contact with universal spirit entities and guides, and intense communication with extraterrestrial intelligences. For them, the New Age involves powerful spiritual energy radiating from the astrological constellations, invisible power saturating our planet as we enter the Age of Aquarius. They see all these things combining to inspire and energize earthly human beings, much as Christians believe the outpouring of the latter rain will do in the last days. The present is a period of spiritual awakening, New Agers say, of discovering one's "higher self" by focusing inward to the "god within us."

Centers, clinics, and channelers

As a result of this new interest, New Age centers such as the Akashic Book Shop in Thousand Oaks, California, and the Yes Bookstore in Washington D.C., have sprung up in virtually every major city. There is such a demand for New Age literature today that one New Age book distributor in the United States recently reported that he has 3,200 bookstores on his customer list.[9]

West Hollywood, California, has probably the largest New Age bookstore in America—The Bodhi Tree, a pair of two-story houses on Melrose Avenue converted into a bookstore. It gets its name from the fact that Siddhartha Gautama (Buddha) was sitting under a bodhi tree when he was inspired with the "Four Noble Truths."[10] Its doors are open twelve hours every day to accommodate customers, who range from movie and TV celebrities to executives, college students, and homemakers. It stocks over twenty-seven thousand New Age titles, in approximately three hundred sections. Topics range from New Age cuisine to New Age sex. If it's New Age you want, you can find it at The Bodhi Tree—magazines, books, crystals, wands, and other New Age paraphernalia.

The rooms are filled with ceiling-high bookcases. On the few walls not covered with books hang pictures of gurus and other spiritual guides. You would be amazed and shocked to see that among the pictures of Gandhi, Sister Teresa, Paramahansa Yogananda, and other gurus is a picture of Christ! New Agers believe that Christ, during those silent years of His youth and young adult life, went to India to study and became a guru to Christianity.

New Age health food stores have come into vogue. New Age holistic health clinics of all kinds have opened up around the country. Many New Age resorts, such as John Denver's "Wind Star" in Colorado, have become popular retreats. And to help people know what is out there in the New Age world, New Age fairs have been organized in many major cities to display products and acquaint you with the movement's beliefs.

Today the channeling business is a multimillion dollar enterprise. Channelers, the new name for the old spirit mediums, are highly sought after for their mediatory consulting services. These modern-day mediums have exchanged their dark, spooky parlors, weird garb, and crystal balls for well-lighted modern consulting offices. Many have master's and Ph.D. degrees in the various disciplines of psychology and other related fields. Their businesses are thriving because people today have a great interest in the future, in life after death, and in consulting with the dead and the spirit entities of the universe.

In 1988 "nearly half of American adults (42 percent)" believed they had been contacted by someone who had died. This was up from 27 percent from a national survey taken eleven years earlier.[11]

A threat to Christianity

Millions of Americans from every walk of life are concerned with inner growth, and they have been experimenting with such things as Eastern meditation and mysticism. The 1990 Gallup poll, *Religion in America, Approaching the Year 2000*, says:

> Few will dispute the fact that the 90's will be a period of severe testing for the churches of America, as they seek to relate to the populace that is increasingly drawn to spirituality, but less enthusiastic about organized religion, which they often find to be irrelevant, unfulfilling, and boring. Of particular concern to the traditional churches is the growing interest among the populous in paranormal, psychic, ghostly and other world experiences, and their susceptibility to movements such as the New Age, which traditionalists believe lead to a worship of self rather than God.[12]

Even more alarming, this Gallup survey shows that the popular beliefs and philosophies of the New Age are just as widespread among Americans who are "deeply religious" in a traditional sense as they are among those who are not. Russell Chandler, a religion writer for the *Los Angeles Times* and author of the book, *Understanding the New Age*, says that "the New Age is probably the most widespread and powerful phenomenon affecting our culture today. In newsbiz, we call it 'hot.'"[13]

The New Age phenomenon is not something we can brush off lightly or ignore. It is dangerous because it strikes at the very heart of our Christian faith—salvation through Jesus Christ and belief in a personal God. In the following pages we will take a closer look at some of these undermining New Age beliefs that can be traced back to the Garden of Eden and that old serpent, the devil. We will see how his candy-coated versions of these forbidden fruits are being sold to us today by his New Age peddlers.

1. Marilyn Ferguson, *The Aquarian Conspiracy* (Los Angeles: J. P. Tarcher, Inc., 1987), 25.
2. *Christian Research Newsletter*, 5 (March/April 1992).
3. Ferguson, *The Aquarian Conspiracy*, 23, 24.
4. Ibid., 13.
5. *Christian Research Newsletter*, 5 (March/April 1992).
6. Johanna Michaelsen, *Like Lambs to the Slaughter* (Eugene, Oreg.: Harvest House Publishers, 1989), 10.
7. Shirley MacLaine, *Going Within: A Guide for Inner Transformation* (New York: Bantam Books, 1989), 29, 30.
8. *Los Angeles Times*, 3 March 1989.
9. "Demystifying New Age Books," *Publishers Weekly*, 24 June 1988, 58, 60.
10. John Snelling, *The Buddhist Handbook* (Rochester, Vt.: Inner Traditions International, Ltd., 1991), 21, 22.
11. Russell Chandler, *Understanding the New Age* (Dallas: Word Publishing, 1988), 20.
12. George Gallup, Jr., *Religion in America—Approaching the Year 2000*, 1990 Report, 10.
13. Chandler, *Understanding the New Age* (dust jacket).

2

Occult TV Programs and Toys

Suppose I were to ask you to go on a scavenger hunt looking for traces of the New Age in your own home. Most likely, one of the last places you would think to look would be in your child's toy box. And although you might correctly single out the "one-eyed monster" in your family room as a possible conduit for New Age programs, would you suspect some of those "innocent" cartoons that your child views several hours a week? Most parents have never sat down to watch a full hour of the cartoons by which their children are entertained day after day. But it might be a good idea to do so in order to become acquainted with the insidious way the occult[1] and New Age beliefs have infiltrated the very programs that are baby-sitting your children.

The New Age propaganda being shown on these programs is forming another foundation for your child's belief and value system. Most of us grew up in a Judeo-Christian culture. Today our children are growing up in a neopagan culture, and TV has become the undeclared educator for the masses. Phil Phillips states, "Today's children are enrolled in a catechism that promotes Eastern religion, new-age philosophies, neopaganism, and the occult."[2]

Children between the ages of two and five, according to A. C. Nielsen Company data, are entertained twenty-eight hours a week by TV. Children between six and eleven years old watch twenty-three and a half hours a week on the average.[3] Even if your child does not view TV at home, he or she will most likely see some of the occult cartoons or programs teaching New Age philosophies at a friend's home or at school. At the very least, he will become knowledgeable about them through reading comics, toy instructions, or just by talking with peers. At one time violence was parents' overriding concern with TV cartoons, but today there is *double* trouble—violence and the New Age philosophies.

Masters of the Universe

Take, for example, "Masters of the Universe"—a program primarily aimed at children featuring muscular, gladiatorlike, supernatural men and women and superhuman creatures with human characteristics. The women in these episodes have hour-glass figures, with scanty, body-tight outfits. For some children, these female characters are their very first introduction to soft-core pornography. The "Masters of the Universe" characters are both good and evil, and the episodes are packed with sorcery, witchcraft, magic, and spells. The hero is "He-Man of the Universe," also called Prince Adam, who lives in Eternia—an eerie similarity to the Adam whom God created in the Garden of Eden. Prince Adam, or He-Man, has his "good" friends—Orco, a midget and hooded ghost who suspends himself in air and performs magic; his pet tiger Cringer, who can be transformed into Battle Cat; and Sorceress, a beautiful young woman who performs white magic and can take the form of a falcon.

He-Man's Battle Cat is an example of how these cartoons subtly expose children to pagan beliefs. It was common in ancient pagan and occult practices for animals, known as "familiars," to possess spirit powers and to help people involved in supernatural activities.[4] Cats especially were considered sacred in pagan cultures such as ancient Egypt. Battle Cat is He-Man's "familiar." He-Man's sister, She-Ra, has a horse, Swift Wind, that also is a "familiar."

Other "good" characters the children watch in this animated program are: Battle Armor He-Man; Teela, a heroic warrior goddess; and Fisto, a hand-to-hand fighter with huge fists of iron. When the evil forces led by Skeletor, the lord of destruction, threaten Prince Adam, he reaches back and pulls a sword from the nape of his neck, utters the magic words "by the power of Greyskull" (this is what is called an "invocation" in the occult world), and transforms himself into "He-Man of the Universe." This ability to transform oneself into another person or creature is also a standard pagan belief.

Just the names of some of the evil warriors led by Skeletor give you an idea of their characters: Beast Man; Evil Henchman; Evil-Lyn; Evil Warrior Goddess; Kobra Khan, master of the snakes. In battle both sides—good and evil forces—employ sorcery and magic. Skeletor and his group use "black magic," while He-Man's "good" friend, Sorceress, uses "white magic."

Princess of Power

She-Ra plays the part of Adora, an ordinary woman, until she transforms herself into the Princess of Power by holding high her sword and pronouncing the words "for the honor of Greyskull." She fights the Horde that has taken control of the planet. She-Ra has a wizard called Light Hope, whom she consults for advice; when needed, her shaman, or spirit guide, appears in the crystal stone of She-Ra's sword. As you can see, this program exposes your child to many occult and pagan concepts.

She-Ra's name is derived from Ra—the ancient Egyptian sun god, also revered as part of Baal worship. She-Ra uses "white magic" and possesses healing powers.

Every program is packed with action and suspense. And while your child is totally absorbed in this kind of entertainment, Satan is gleefully filling his mind with knowledge of occult beliefs and practices as well as familiarizing him with the terminology.

Unfortunately, the influence of these programs does not stop when you turn off the TV. The cartoons have spawned a number of corresponding books, comics, and toy characters that are not as delightful and innocent as they may appear. In fact, they are downright dangerous and could be the very things that will encourage your child to experiment later with more sophisticated forms of the satanic occult world.

Danger in the toy box

Some children's toys are not designed to teach a moral lesson, good or bad—skates, dolls, trucks, and cars, for example. Other toys are based on Christian themes or Bible characters. But some toys are warlike, such as guns, knives, bows and arrows. And some toys are mystic in nature because of their associations with occult TV programs for children. In this section, we will look at this last category of toys.

After a child has been exposed to the TV cartoons promoting occult ideas, once he understands the plots, he will want to get the toy characters of his favorite programs. The natural next step is to play out what he has seen those characters do on TV—combating and surviving in a world of demons, witches, and wizards.

Here are the instructions that Mattel gives to the child who buys a Skeletor. (Skeletor, if you don't know, has a very muscular body, webbed feet, and a yellow-green skeleton face with a hood on his head. He carries a sword and a scepter with a ram's head on top. The ram's head, of course, has always been a symbol of Satan.) Now for the instructions:

> When you put on your Skeletor helmet and your armored belt you become transformed into an agent of Evil. Use your power sword and shield to combat good. With your mystical Ram's head scepter, you will be able to call forth the denizens of darkness.[5]

You might say, "Well, I don't allow my children to watch programs like 'The Masters of the Universe,' and I certainly wouldn't buy them a toy like Skeletor." That's good, and Satan knows that he may not be able to reach your children this way. So he has wrapped some of his evil seeds in different, more subtle packages such as the Smurfs, My Little Pony, and the Care-Bears.

The Smurfs

The Smurfs, tiny blue creatures, are from a village in make-believe land. They all seem so cute and innocent looking—but the program is laced through and through with New Age themes and beliefs. When the Smurfs, or their human friends, get into trouble, to whom do they turn?

You're right. They turn to Papa Smurf, who is a wizard. He practices sorcery and witchcraft and can come up with a spell potion or mantra (a word or phrase that supposedly has magical power) or some other form of magic to help them out of their predicament. Mantras are used by the Hindus to help them prepare for meditation—and Eastern meditation, which I will discuss in a later chapter, is something you may not want your children to become involved with.

Papa Smurf often refers to Beelzebub, one of the names given to

Satan in the Bible. In one episode, a medieval village was being manipulated by a burly thief with a magic flute. Nothing could stop the evil effects of the flute on the village people—until a white-bearded wizard dressed in a dark blue robe told two young heroes that the only hope was to obtain and utilize a second magical flute from the same Smurfs who had made the original one. Through an advanced magic spell called hypnokinesis, the wizard transferred the two humans to the land of the Smurfs. Papa Smurf was able to make another flute with greater magical powers to counteract the original flute. In the climactic scene a dramatic struggle took place between the two flutists until the evil one finally collapsed. The subtle answer to problems on this program seems to be magic—white magic.

My Little Pony

My Little Pony is a children's program that you would probably never think to classify as New Age, but it is. These little pastel-colored ponies with long shiny manes and tails experience tranquility in their meadows until the peace is broken by evil dragons from the sky. These dragons capture and transport the ponies to their master, Scorpion, who is half goat and half man. The master then converts the ponies, through magic, into dragons to pull his chariot of darkness.

Those ponies that escape the dragons run to seek help from a wizard who gives them a piece of the rainbow. This is supposed to give them power against Scorpion. Here again, we have plots dealing with the occult and wizards. As your child watches, he or she is becoming more and more familiar with occult terminology and conditioned to accept the use of mystical spirit guides and magic as a way to survive and to gain success and power.

Care Bears

The Care Bears are some of the most innocent, cuddly-looking stuffed animals you can imagine. Many moms and grandmas have bought their children and grandchildren these irresistible little stuffed animals, never suspecting the evil influence they may have on them. The children adore them so much they often refuse to be separated from them even at bedtime and cuddle them all night long.

The Care Bears, like the Smurfs and Ponies, also have their corresponding toys and books. There are seven cuddly Care Bears, each one a different color with his particular name identified on his white chest and stomach. Their personalities match their names—Tenderhearts, Love-a-Lot, Friend, Share-Bear, etc.

In the cartoons, the Care Bears endeavor to teach the children good, moral lessons such as sharing or being friendly. But that fact makes the danger all the more subtle. For in the process of coming to that little kernel of good at the end, the Care Bear scenarios often take your children through acts of sorcery or scenes of witchery and demonic ventures—exposing them again and again to the occult, to pagan symbols and beliefs. One of the beliefs subtly taught by the Care Bears comes from the Hindu religion. This is the belief that if you concentrate your energies on one part of your body, as the Care Bears do with their "Care-Bear Stare," you can perform white magic. In these popular children's programs, black magic is usually performed by the evil forces, whereas white magic is performed by the good forces.

Whenever I speak on the dangers of occult TV cartoons and toys, it is both amusing and alarming to see the reaction of parents. The children all know every character and occult situation on the TV programs I mention. Their eyes light up as I use some of the actual toy characters as visual aids. Many of the parents cannot believe how much their children know about these things.

Bucky O'Hare

Another cartoon with New Age overtones is Bucky O'Hare, a rabbit commander in charge of the spaceship *Righteous Indignation.* Bucky, along with Jenny, a supercat woman, fights against the evil Toad Empire using sorcery, powers of concentration, and out-of-body experiences. Jenny also has a "third eye," which she uses for concentration. The "third eye" is part of the Hindu belief that everyone has a hidden eye located in his or her forehead that has supernatural sight and power.

Captain Planet

This would appear on the surface to be an acceptable program, since the main theme is fighting evil environmental forces that want to pollute and destroy our planet. This TV program is set in the 1990s, and the good characters, the "Planeteers," are all sharp, ethnic, college-age young people. The enemies of earth are rough-looking hooligans such as Duke Nukem, a character who looks like he is made of stones, although he is really made of nuclear waste. He gains his strength from radiation, which he uses to fight Captain Planet and the Planeteers. The five Planeteers, three young men and two young women, have been chosen from different parts of the world by "Gaia," the Spirit of the Earth. (*Gaia* is a New Age term that comes from Greek mythology and refers to the goddess of the earth.)

Gaia has given each teenager a magic ring by which he or she can call up a specific power to combat the destroyers of the environment: Kwame, the African, uses the power of the earth; Linka, the Russian, commands the power of the wind; Gi, the Asian, controls the forces of water; MaTi, the Latin, uses the power of heart to communicate telepathically with Gaia and the Planeteers.

Once again we are dealing with the occult. These five Planeteers, by joining the powers of their magic rings, can materialize Captain Planet, the "superman" who combats those who pollute and destroy our planet. Captain Planet's key phrase is, "The planet is ours; the power is yours." "The power is yours" is repeated several times during each program. This suggestion, planted in the minds of children, can lead them to look inward to themselves for the source of power, instead of looking to Jesus.

Paw Paw Bears

"If you get in trouble, who do you call? The Paw Paw Bears." So goes the TV introduction. These cute little bears, much like the Care-Bears, appear as native Indians and are always there to help those in need. But Dark Paw and his friends try to interfere. Dark Paw's weapon is his scepter (with an eagle's head mounted on top), which he uses to zap people. Princess Paw Paw uses the magic amulet on her necklace to bring to life the Totem Bear (a large wooden totem pole–like bear). This is yet another TV cartoon that introduces children to occult beliefs and practices while entertaining them. Satan is no dummy. He is indoctrinating a whole new generation through these types of children's programs.

Parents, you have a responsibility to know what you allow your children to watch. Satan is trying to fill their fresh, impressionable minds with his lies. Not every program within these cartoon series is blatant with New Age themes, of course, but over the course of time, these series cover just about every basic occult belief and practice there is to know.

Teenage Mutant Ninja Turtles

The Teenage Mutant Ninja Turtles are among the most popular of the children's TV programs. Most of the children I've talked to during my lectures know all about them. These four turtles, who live in the sewers of New York City along with their ninja master Splinter, were accidentally saturated with a mysterious chemical, causing them to grow to their present human size.

The turtles fight city crime, becoming good friends with April O'Neil, a crime reporter for Channel 3 TV News. The harmful part about the program is that it glamorizes the violent martial art of ninja. Satan is so clever that he uses characters such as turtles to downplay this occult and pagan martial art. The program also introduces Eastern meditation and spiritualism, which, until a dozen years ago, Western children knew little about.

Some may not realize that many of the armed and unarmed martial arts such as ninja, karate, tae kwon do, and kung fu are influenced by such Eastern religions as Taoism and Zen Buddhism and "are practiced as a means of spiritual development."[6] For instance, Splinter (the rat) can make his old Japanese ninja master, Yoshi, appear out of the flames of the fire simply by meditating. And the wisdom that Splinter receives from this ninja spirit is passed on to the turtles. In turn, the four turtles, with their eyes closed, meditating together, can produce out of the flames of a campfire the image of Splinter, their ninja master. Splinter tells them such things as, "I am proud of you, my sons. Tonight you have learned the final and greatest truth of the Ninja, that ultimate mastery comes not of the body, but of the mind."[7] This is occult philosophy.

The influence of Zen Buddhism and Taoism on ninja and other martial arts is explained in this quote:

> This influence has resulted in a strong emphasis on the mental and spiritual state of the practitioner, a state in which the rationalizing and calculating functions of the mind are suspended so that the mind and body can react immediately as a unit, reflecting the changing situation around the combatant. When this state is perfected, the everyday experience of the dualism of subject and object vanishes. Since this mental and physical state is also central to Taoism and Zen, and must be experienced to be grasped, many of their adher-

ents practice the martial arts as a part of their philosophical and spiritual training.[8]

In the turtles' own words, "Hey, Dude, this is no cartoon." I understand that remark to mean, "This is not pretend or play stuff. This is the real thing."

When you take the time to watch one of the Ninja Turtles' programs or videos or read one of their booklets, you will realize it is serious—very serious. In fact, it is eternally serious because it could be the turning point in your child's life at which he replaces his Christian religious beliefs for those of the Eastern pagan world.

Violence on children's TV programs

Violence on children's TV cartoon programs is the norm today rather than the exception; cartoons are five times more violent than the shows that appear on prime time. During the Saturday morning cartoon time, an average of seventeen violent acts take place each hour. And on the animated series, "Teenage Mutant Ninja Turtles," this number jumps to thirty-four violent acts per hour.[9] Cartoons have traditionally been humorous. However, today's cartoons have been more correctly named "wartoons" because of all the violence they contain. Given the number of hours a child views these programs, concern is rising over the effect of desensitization on their lives. Will they become desensitized to violence in real life in the same way that they become to the violence on television?

Besides the obvious violence fed to your child by TV, the programs deliberately serve up numerous, more subtle messages: People responsible for violent acts are rarely held responsible or punished on TV. The good guys generally use the same methods of warfare and revenge as the bad guys. The family unit is rarely portrayed as the norm. More likely than not, advice on how to cope with life situations is given by someone other than a family member. TV places an exaggerated emphasis on beauty, with the subtle message that if you're beautiful, you're OK. TV tends to promote stereotyping of foreigners, minorities, women, and certain occupations.

But perhaps one of the most insidious dangers for your child is the attempt to educate him and involve him in the occult and in

Eastern beliefs and philosophies. The old serpent has a well-thought-out marketing strategy for peddling his candied apples.

First, through TV, he introduces your children to occult and spiritualist beliefs and practices while he is entertaining them with fast-moving, highly entertaining, suspense-filled adventure laced with sorcery, witchery, and magic. Each half-hour session at the feet of the entertainment box not only reinforces the "lessons" being taught, but also conditions the child to accept occult terminology and practices as normal. In these cartoons, your child is taught such practices as "how to protect yourself by using spells," "how to cast spells," "how to concentrate your energies in order to move or bend objects," and the art of levitation—lifting a person or thing supernaturally.

After planting these seeds of evil in their young brains, Satan seeks to reinforce them through correlated follow-up books and toys.

Ghost Writer

The children's program "Ghost Writer" revolves around four schoolchildren who befriend a lost spirit. This "ghost" then helps them solve mysteries by communicating to them through codes and written words. They ask him questions by writing on paper or on the computer. He answers by making words appear on the computer, in the air, or by rearranging preexisting letters—similar to the way the Ouija board operates.

The kids are excited about this "cool" partnership they have with the ghost. They form a special club, The Ghostwriter Team, and only those who have personally been written to by Ghost Writer can belong. Children watching TV at home are encouraged to participate in solving the mysteries during a section of the program called "time to do the word thing." They write down the clues and try to solve the mystery as the program continues. At the end they are encouraged to write for their own Ghost Writer sticker. It's easy to see how some children could become intrigued with an invisible communicator; instead of being frightened by such contact, they would regard it as a special privilege.

Parents often overlook or fail to realize the fact that most young children believe everything they are told, especially if the person giving the information is an authority figure. Consequently, they accept everything they see on TV as being real or the truth.

Until a child is seven years old, he sees TV as reality. He views everything in a literal sense. . . . No matter how much a parent tries to explain to a child that what he (or she) sees on TV isn't real, the child simply doesn't have the developmental capabilities to comprehend that information.[10]

The steady impulses of the TV program itself—the constant motion, the change of scenes, and the resulting flashes of color every few seconds—cause the brain to release a chemical that, in pharmaceutical terms, would be considered a depressant. This brain-induced drug allows children to appear glued to a TV set, sometimes watching it for as long as three hours without a bathroom break. This is the same type of chemical that, when given in larger doses, can result in a drugged state often used for brainwashing purposes![11]

I have touched here on only a few of the many TV programs that are subtly influencing your child. Much more could be said about the effects of TV in general—the desensitization to violence, the suppression of creativity, the use of TV as an escape mechanism, the diminishing of the attention span, the changing of family values, and the dulling of spiritual senses. However, with the New Age influence so prevalent in these children's programs, even the most complacent parent should feel concerned.

In the next chapter we'll focus on another area that is even more dangerous to children than TV cartoons and toys!

---

1. The word *occult* comes from the Latin word *occultus*, which means "hidden" or "unseen." In Bible times all those practices involving Satanism, divination, sorcery, astrology, and contacting the dead were strongly condemned by God. Therefore, those who practiced them had to do so in secret in order to escape prosecution.

2. Phil Phillips, *Saturday Morning Mind Control* (Nashville: Thomas Nelson Publishers, 1991), 109.

3. Ibid., vii.

4. Ibid., 115.

5. Texe Marrs, *Dark Secrets of the New Age* (Westchester, Ill.: Crossway Books, 1987), 244.

6. *The New Encyclopaedia Britannica*, s.v. "martial arts."

7. B. B. Hiller, *Teenage Mutant Ninja Turtles* (New York: Dell Publishing, 1990), 65.

8. *The New Encyclopaedia Britannica*, s.v. "martial arts."

9. Phillips, *Saturday Morning Mind Control*, 49, 50.
10. Ibid., 15.
11. Ibid., 102.

3

New Age
Occult Games

As detrimental as many TV programs are for children, the occult electronic games that are so popular today are even worse in terms of spiritual and character damage. They are worse because a child or young adult becomes directly involved, actually interacting with the characters on the screen.

The most popular electronic game systems are Super Nintendo, Sega Genesis, Atari, and the portable unit, Game Boys. The vast majority of electronic games are involved with occult themes— sports being a major exception. Most electronic games contain sorcery, witchcraft, spells, demons, magic, or brutal violence. These games hold an unbelievable fascination for kids of all ages, from preschoolers to "big kids" in their twenties and thirties. Nintendo "has found its way into eleven million U.S. homes" and "has become a complete entertainment system for the whole family."[1]

Interview with a twelve-year-old

Recently I interviewed Tom, a bright twelve-year-old, while he was playing Super Mario II and Castlevania in his home. Tom, slender and above average height for his age, was dressed in a tank top and shorts and was barefooted. He told me that just about every kid in the church school he attended had electronic games at home. Tom's friend had over two hundred games, and even Tom's three-year-old cousin owned three Nintendo games of his own. When asked why he liked the games so much, Tom said that playing them gave him the sense of having "power" and being in "control." Little wonder, then, that many kids, especially those whose world is so full of uncertainty or out of control, are drawn to a means of experiencing "power" and "control." As I watched, Tom "zapped" about five hundred bad guys and other evil characters in about fifteen minutes. He pointed out that you can earn bonuses while playing the game that will allow you to use different forms of magic to defeat your enemy.

Magazines are published to explain the strategy of these electronic games and to help the players understand all their options and how to use them. These options may include any or all the methods and evil sources that "real" witches and wizards use. Once again, kids learn and assimilate the lessons of witchery and the world of darkness while being entertained.

Nintendo addiction

At a church where I gave a presentation on the dangers of the New Age movement, Marti, an active young mother, and her husband, Bill, approached me to tell of the following experience they had with their then nine-year-old daughter, Jenny, and her Nintendo set.

After Jenny had repeatedly pleaded for a Nintendo, Mom and Dad finally gave in and bought her one along with some video games. Jenny became proficient at the games and played them for hours at a time—sometimes for as long as five hours at one sitting! Within six weeks Jenny's character had changed from the sweet, respectful, obedient Christian child she had been to another personality. Whenever her parents called her for supper or reminded her to do her homework or to practice the piano, Jenny was actually unable to hear them. It was obvious that Nintendo had become an obsession with her. Marti said, "It seemed to us that she was in a trance, totally absorbed in her Nintendo and oblivious to her surroundings."

Her parents put Jenny's TV and Nintendo system in the basement laundry room. Soon they noticed something peculiar about the atmosphere surrounding the area where the Nintendo was located. Marti began to sense a demonic presence and had a strong suspicion that Jenny was becoming possessed. Jenny was spending all her Sunday afternoons indoors, staying up until eleven o'clock at night playing Mario Brothers I and II, Zelda, and The Legend of Zelda. (Zelda, by the way, is one of the most occultic and demonic electric games around.)

Her parents decided to confiscate the controls, but Jenny found them and began playing her Nintendo secretly. When the parents found out, Bill disconnected all the game's cables and hid them; Jenny found them and put the whole system back together again.

"How she figured it out," Marti says, "I do not know. But it does show how highly motivated and addicted she was to Nintendo." Bill decided to find out for himself what these games were all about. After playing two games with Jenny, he was convinced that the terms used throughout the games were occultic and demonic. So Jenny's parents approached her with the idea of getting rid of the Nintendo and games.

At first she became hysterical at the thought. But her mother told her, "Jenny, I have been praying all afternoon about what to say to you. Would you agree to go to your room and pray to Jesus yourself?"

Jenny spent about an hour in her room. When she came downstairs, she had tears in her eyes, and she said, "Mom, I think Jesus wants me to get rid of this." That was two years ago; today Jenny, Marti, and Bill are once again a happy Christian family.

Demonic board games

You would think that if someone wished to purchase an occult game, he would have to go to a special game store that featured adult, mystical games. But on the contrary, you can buy just about any occult or magical toy or game you wish at children's toy stores—games such as Hero Quest by Milton Bradley, a "high adventure in a world of magic" for ages ten to adult. The description on the box of this game states in part: "One of you will play the part of Zargo, the evil sorcerer. With your mutant monster forces, you'll plot against the heroes. Watch them fall prey to cunning." Other players are Barbarian, Elf, Wizard, and Dwarf.

Parker Brothers' old Ouija board, the mystifying oracle board that kids like to dabble with by asking questions, can be found in the toy store alongside all the other games on the shelf. The alluring lines on the Ouija game box say, "Explore the mysteries of mental telepathy and the subconscious with this time-tested favorite." Some of you who dabbled with this occult game in your youth know that this is no mere game. It is satanic.

However, the occult game most sought after today is Dungeons and Dragons. And in terms of mental stability and Christian spirituality, it is also probably the most dangerous pastime in which anyone can indulge. Dungeons and Dragons places the players in contact with demonic spirits and the occult in a world filled with magic, sorcery, killing, robbery, maiming, bloodshed, sexual abuse, rape, hatred, and the casting of magic spells. It is a mind game of evil strategy in which players work their way up through different levels of skills and abilities. As they gain higher levels, they acquire new spells and magic. But these take time and patience to acquire.[2] Pat Pulling, mother of a boy who committed suicide as a result of his involvement with Dungeons and Dragons, describes the game manual as containing "detailed descriptions of killing, satanic human sacrifice, assassination, sadism, premeditated murder, and curses of insanity."[3]

Bob, a young man I met at a camp meeting, told me he was introduced to Dungeons and Dragons by one of his Christian friends when he was fourteen years old. His friend was quite knowledgeable about the game and always played the part of the Dungeon Master. Bob, at one point, managed to acquire an army of thirty or so, which gave him a euphoric feeling and sense of power. The game became so real to him that he actually felt he was living out the game in his real life. Then, in the game, he was killed along with his whole army. This threw him into a deep depression for about two weeks. His friend, who had introduced him to the game, later committed suicide.

Dungeons and Dragons not only fills the mind with occult images, it destroys reality. It can become a consuming, addictive, and potentially dangerous pastime. Christian parents should be aware of these subtle dangers that can destroy not only their child's spirituality, but may also destroy his life.

The National Coalition on Television Violence has linked the game to 50 suicides and murders since 1979. A 16-year-old New York boy, David K. Ventiquattro, was convicted of killing a fellow D&D player following a game. He told police that the younger boy had become "evil" in the fantasy, and it was his role to "extinguish the evil."[4]

Touching the palate
So, as a parent, what should you do about these dangerous TV

programs, games, and toys? What should those of us do who are not parents?

If you have children, it would be well for you to become aware of the New Age and the occult influences to which they are exposed. Limit the number of hours you allow your children to watch television. Then monitor the programs they watch. If the children are old enough, you may want to view the program with them, explaining and pointing out the pagan and occult teachings.

Encourage your children to read good books if they are old enough, or read books to them. Break the TV addiction by replacing it with something educational and of moral value. Get rid of all the occult toys, books, and games in your home. You may even consider getting rid of the TV itself.

Proverbs 22:6 says, "Train up a child in the way he should go: and when he is old, he will not depart from it." This verse became more meaningful to me when I discovered that in Hebrew there is a very close link between the verb meaning "train up" and the noun meaning "palate, roof of the mouth, gums."[5] This connection possibly referred to the method Hebrew mothers used to wean their children from breast-feeding. A mother would take table food and chew it until it was broken up and ready to swallow. Then she would put her finger into her mouth, take out some food, and introduce it to her child by touching it to his palate. At once the child's digestive juices would begin to flow, and he would swallow automatically.

In time the child developed a natural liking for the food to which he was introduced at an early age on his mother's lap. Just as we still get excited about savoring Mother's home cooking even as adults, children instructed in the things of the Lord when they are infants will long for them when they are grown. The spiritual lesson and question is: With what are we touching the palate of our children—occult TV cartoons, books, and toys? Or are we touching their senses with spiritual themes from the Bible? What will they turn to when they are old enough to make decisions on their own?

Let's fight magic with the power of God's Word. Let's touch their palates with the Bread of Life so that the candy-coated rotten apples that Satan is offering them will hold no allure.

Now that we've seen the adverse influence of TV programs and occult games on children, let's take a look at the sort of sophisticated packaging job Satan has done to promote these same lies to a more "mature" audience.

1. Joan Hake Robie, *Turmoil in the Toybox, II* (Lancaster, Pa.: Starburst Publishers, 1989), 160.
2. *Dragon Warrior Strategy Guide* (published by Nintendo of America, Inc., and Tokuma Shoten, 1989), 26.
3. Robie, *Turmoil in the Toybox II*, 150.
4. Ibid., 149.
5. *The New Brown, Driver, and Briggs Hebrew and English Lexicon of the Old Testament* (Grand Rapids, Mich.: Baker Book House, 1981), 335.

CHAPTER

4

Entertainment

In my opinion, the motion picture and television industries have done more to change the morals and values of people than any other single factor in the history of modern times.

Movies can take us back into history or project us far into the future. They can reconstruct historical events and create the wildest fantasies imaginable. They help form our political ideologies and moral values. They shape the way we dress, the way we talk, the way we eat, and most significantly, the way we think. The motion picture industry, whether movies or TV, has been a major source for information, entertainment, and a means of bringing the world closer to us. At the same time, both these media have had phenomenal success in introducing new ideas and concepts that are eroding or replacing traditional Christian values.

New Agers in the entertainment business know this all too well and are exploiting this industry to the maximum. Shirley MacLaine heads the long list of stars and celebrities who hold New Age views, a list that includes Helen Reddy, Lisa Bonet, Tina Turner, Phil Donahue, Oprah Winfrey, Linda Evans, John Denver, Burt Reynolds, Clint Eastwood, and Sharon Gless. Sharon Gless, upon receiving a 1987 Emmy Award for her role on the series "Cagney and Lacey," told tens of millions who were watching on TV that she owed her success to "Lazarus," her spirit entity.

Some of the most prominent movie producers and directors today are New Agers, including Steven Spielberg and George Lucas. What Walt Disney was to American families in the forties, fifties, and sixties, Lucas and Spielberg are to the seventies, eighties, and nineties. These men have become New Age evangelists, indoctrinating millions through their films. Whereas most of the present adult generation were raised in a Judeo-Christian society, today's children are growing up in a secular and occult society.

Eastern religious beliefs and Native American psychic phenomena, concepts that seemed strange and foreign to the Western mind a few years ago, are now not only common knowledge but practiced and espoused by thousands of Americans.

For the last couple of decades, religious leaders and others have been expressing concern about the movies that Hollywood produces because of the great effect they have on the general populace. As a result of public pressure, the movie industry devised ratings to indicate appropriateness for different types of viewers: "G" for general audiences, "PG" for parental guidance, "PG 13" (some material may not be appropriate for children under 13), "R" for restricted, and most recently, "NC 17" (no children under 17). Unfortunately, few people pay attention to the ratings. If they want to see a film, they see it no matter what the rating is. If it has foul language, explicit sex, violence, horror, or New Age themes, it matters little to many viewers. People seem to think that what they see or hear at the movies or on television has little or no effect on them. But they are dead wrong, for everything that is allowed to enter our minds becomes stored information. This is the information bank that we draw from to determine our values, beliefs, and lifestyles.

One young man said to me recently, "I can go to the movies, watch a video, or see a film on television and take from that film whatever I want. I can leave the rest. I know what's right and wrong. I know what's biblical and what isn't. I know what is fantasy and what is reality. I'm an intelligent adult and can handle it."

Our minds are capable of determining what is right and what is wrong—based on the information we have previously stored in them that enables us to make that kind of an evaluation. Nevertheless, we cannot just discard the negative information and influences we allow to enter the mind like we would a container we put out in the trash. These negative things remain in the mind along with the positive. The mind is like a computer; everything received through the senses is stored and available for recall. So we must be discriminating in what we allow to enter.

In this chapter I will not deal with horror movies such as the Freddie Krueger *Nightmare on Elm Street* series or the *Friday the 13th* films, all of which were R-rated. I will not be commenting on some of the extreme violence and adult language in the films of Arnold Schwarzenegger, Chuck Norris, or Sylvester Stallone. Nor will I critique the NC-17 films that present nudity and explicit adult sexual situations, as bad as these are. For these are films that most Christians would, or should, be able to discern as unsuitable for their viewing.

But the films most likely to be viewed by Christians are those that carry a PG or PG-13 rating, films such as Steven Spielberg's *Close Encounters of the Third Kind, Raiders of the Lost Ark, Indiana Jones and the Temple of Doom,* or *Always.* Or the George Lucas films: *Star Wars, Return of the Jedi, The Empire Strikes Back,* and *Willow.* Or Ron Howard's *Cocoon* and its sequel. Films such as *The Karate Kid Part I* and *Part II, Ghostbusters I* and *II, The Butcher's Wife, Ghost,* and all the *Ninja* films that have recently been produced.

I purchased a book at B. Dalton bookstores, available to anyone, which lists more than nineteen thousand films and eight thousand videos along with a short description and rating of each one. Much of the information one would need to determine the suitability of any particular film can be found in that book; a person doesn't have to view a movie in order to critique it.

While violence and explicit sex are obvious in a film, what may not be so obvious is that all the above-mentioned movies, as well as many others, are laced through and through with New Age teachings: reincarnation, life after death in the form of disembodied spirits, channeling, clairvoyance, psychic phenomena, UFOs, ESP, and mystical meditation. These elements are not in these movies by happenstance. They're there by design. It is part of Satan's master plan to deceive the human race and destroy its faith in God. The enemy has infiltrated the minds of producers and directors to market pagan doctrines and erroneous demonic concepts to Westerners and Christians in particular.

In the *Karate Kid* series, Eastern religious beliefs are introduced in a very subtle way through the martial arts discipline of karate—subtle, because while you are being entertained you are also being indoctrinated in occult philosophies. While your defenses are down, New Age lies are being fed to you.

Miagi, an Oriental handyman and martial arts master, transforms skinny Daniel into a karate champion, coaching him and teaching him occult concepts. "What is within you," Miagi tells Daniel, is always right. "The Buddha provides," he plants in Daniel's mind (and in the viewer's mind as well). In *Karate Kid Part III* Daniel even worships the spirit of a bonsai tree! This is pantheism.

Gandhi is a film produced specifically to promote Hinduism to the Western mind. The Indian government was so interested in this project that it invested one-third of the movie's budget of nine million English pounds to ensure its production. *Ghandi* was the pride and joy of India's elite society; at last the West would see the more palatable side of their religion. Without question the film was a high religious and political priority for the Hindu government.[1]

An analytical look at *ET*, a tremendously popular film a few years ago, reveals many parallels to the story of Christ's life. ET has supernatural powers. He heals and even resurrects himself, just as Jesus did. And when ET finally leaves this earth, he allows only Elliott, his young friend, and the close circle of kids who have befriended him, to see him off in his spaceship—just as Jesus allowed only His close followers to see Him leave the earth. ET is a demon lookalike, but introduced in such innocent settings that children adore him. In fact, *ET* has become an all-time box office blockbuster.

The sequels of *Superman* are woven around themes that increasingly resemble the life of Christ—Superman coming from outer space as a baby, possessing supernatural powers, and fighting for truth and justice.

These "gospels from outer space" had subtle parallels to Christianity, but they were far from promoting Christian beliefs and values. Other films have since been released that have also promoted New Age themes, but these were among the first.

George Lucas's *Willow* is an interesting film, to say the least. Besides witchery and sorcery, it presupposes that the "myths portrayed in the film exist in all of us." The movie was, according to Lucas, a microcosm of what is inside those who watched the film. All the little creatures and characters in this mythical epic are Lucas's "best friends." George Lucas's guru, Joseph Campbell, believes that myths are representations of inner realities and truths.

These movies entertain you with vivid, action-packed scenes and graphic demonic power struggles using magic and spells. As a Christian, you may not believe or practice the occult. However, the more you watch such movies, the less objectionable these demonic practices will seem. The movies are perfect setups for Satan, for while he is entertaining you, he is at the same time filling your mind with his sophistries.

Cocoon and *Cocoon: The Return* carry the themes of life after death and transferring life from one person to another. *Field of Dreams* stars Kevin Costner as a novice farmer in Iowa who hears the "voice" of a deceased baseball specter that convinces him to convert his cornfield into a baseball diamond in order to bring back to life the legendary baseball star, Shoeless Joe Jackson. In recent years, there has been a large number of life-after-death films contradicting the scriptural teaching that "the dead know not any thing. . . . Neither have they any more a portion for ever in any thing that is done under the sun" (Ecclesiastes 9:5, 6). Films greatly influence the way you think. The more you expose yourself to movies with New Age themes, the greater will be the change in you. It may take years, and it may be a gradual change, but be assured, it will happen.

In *The Butcher's Wife*, Demi Moore plays an innocent, unassuming wife who glamorizes her apparently natural clairvoyant powers, a heathen practice condemned by God (see Deuteronomy 18:10-12).

Ghostbusters I and *II* are scary comedies with very serious demonic implications. Bill Murray, Dan Aykroyd, and company drive around the Big Apple, flushing out ghosts and spirits. It may have been great fun, but ghosts and spirits are no laughing matter. In fact, in *Ghostbusters II*, the cruel, sixteenth-century king, Vigo the Carpathian, whose painting is in the Metropolitan Museum of Art, speaks to the painter who is restoring his painting.

"I, Vigo, the scourge of Carpathia, the sorrow of Moldavia, command you! . . . On a mountain of skulls in a castle of pain, I sat on a throne of blood!" Vigo declares, his voice booming in the large gallery. "What was, will be; what is, will be no more. Now is the season of evil. Find me a child that I might live again!"[2] Then bolts of eerie, orange-red, electrical energy–like, crackling light shoot from Vigo's eyes into Janosz's eyes. Janosz is horrified, screams, and falls to his knees.

Films have a way of involving their viewers emotionally; you must keep reminding yourself that it is only a movie. Nevertheless you are being sensitized and conditioned to the evil world of the occult. Herein lies the danger.

A classic example of how movies subtly introduce New Age beliefs is the popular film *Ghost*. Its all-star cast—Demi Moore, Patrick Swayze, and Whoopi Goldberg—alone excited interest. In the film, Swayze is killed by a mugger but doesn't realize it at the moment and gives chase to his assailant, who gets away. Returning to the scene of the crime, Swayze sees himself dead and realizes that he's now a ghost. He can see and hear what the people around him are saying, but they can't see or hear him.

His grieving girlfriend is in danger, and he frantically tries to warn her, but doesn't succeed very well in his disembodied state until he comes across a storefront channeler, Whoopi Goldberg, who allows Swayze to use her as his medium to communicate messages to Demi. (This is known as "transchanneling.")

The story line is a tender tale of love, warm and at the same time dramatic. Swayze's frustration in his attempt to reach Moore, his girlfriend, is suspenseful. And all the while the viewer is being exposed to the art of levitation and moving objects through the means of intense mind concentration (psychokinesis). The movie strongly introduces the concept of life after death and justifies the use of both conscious and transchannelers.[3] The climax scene is a very clever and appealing portrayal of a transchanneling encounter. Swayze, Goldberg, and Moore are in the same room. Patrick wants so much to be able to hold Demi Moore one more time, but he can do this only if Whoopi Goldberg allows his disembodied spirit to possess her. At this point, the viewers' emotions and expectations heighten. As the theme of "Unchained Melody" plays in the background, Whoopi Goldberg (inhabited by the spirit of Swayze) draws close to Moore. They touch, and then the cameras play tricks with your eyes as Whoopi disappears and Patrick comes into view.

Such themes in movies are subtly conditioning your mind to accept New Age beliefs and practices. These scenes leave indelible impressions on your mind. Scripts are carefully prepared, moods are studied so that you relax your defenses and allow yourself to be not only entertained but also gradually brainwashed into accepting New Age occult themes. Such films are a primary means through which Satan chills your Christian fervor and enthusiasm, gradually eroding and changing your religious beliefs. Of course, this doesn't happen at one sitting or even two, but the more you willingly sit to be fed with entertainment of this nature, the more your spirituality will be adversely affected.

The powers of Matthew Star

"The Power of Matthew Star" is a series that gives credence and respectability to the practice of mental telepathy (communication between minds) and psychokinesis (movement of objects through the power of the mind). The hero, a handsome young teenager, is actually an alien, the son of royalty from the planet Quadrus. Brought to planet Earth by his guardian to escape the conquerors of his planet, Matthew awaits the maturing of his powers of telepathy and psychokinesis so that he can return to rescue his people. In the meantime, he uses whatever powers he possesses to help those in need or to escape from those who seek to harm him. Each episode displays telepathy and psychokinesis as powers that are used on the side of good in its fight against evil. Nevertheless, it is a subtle New Age attempt to nullify negative perceptions about such practices.

The Waltons

Even the squeaky-clean "Waltons" sometimes present New Age philosophies, as in the episode about a falling star that seems to affect the lives of different family members. Or the program in which a little girl talks to flowers and asks if flowers can talk. She is told, "If we learned to listen, we could hear a lot of things." When her pet dies, she asks what death is, and the answer is given: "Death is like closing your eyes. Only instead of the darkness, you see the light." (People with near-death experiences give accounts of seeing a bright light.)

There is no question in my mind that TV and movies reflect a subtle master plan to gradually reeducate our thinking from Judeo-Christian concepts of life to New Age principles of the occult. This is not just happenstance; Satan is behind it all.

Quantum Leap

"Quantum Leap" (a phrase adopted from New Age terminology)

entertains as the main character is sent on missions to change history. In order to do this, he is transformed to appear in the lives of those whose historical events he must change. His spirit guide, who assists him, is a deceased friend who appears as a hologram that only he can see.

Of course, we all know that none of this really happens . . . or do we? Most of us do not believe in reincarnation or in ghosts. But wait. The attention-gripping way in which the scripts are written and their entertaining scenarios could, in time, lead one to wonder about or even believe in these occult phenomena.

New Age thinking is the craze today, not only in the secular world but with some Christians as well. A new Gallup survey shows that belief in many paranormal and psychic experiences is just as widespread among Americans who are deeply religious in a traditional sense as those who are not.[4]

Through Scripture we know that someday Satan will attempt to deceive Christians by appearing as Christ. The apostle Paul says that Satan masquerades as an angel of light (see 2 Corinthians 11:14). It is very likely that he will appear as a supernatural extraterrestrial, bringing healing to the sick and messages of peace to world leaders, being understood by all the language groups in the world. Through our senses, through increasing familiarity with such ideas, we are being conditioned to accept extraterrestrials. Will you be deceived?

Isaiah 33:14-17 relates to this topic. "The sinners in Zion are afraid; fearfulness hath surprised the hypocrites. Who among us shall dwell with the devouring fire? who among us shall dwell with everlasting burnings?" (verse 14). Zion represents the church, and the hypocrites are church members! "Everlasting burning" would refer to the presence of God. The question is: Who—even among those in the church—will be able to live in God's presence?

The answer is given in verse 15: "He that walketh righteously, and speaketh uprightly; he that despiseth the gain of oppressions, that shaketh his hands from holding of bribes, that stoppeth his ears from hearing of blood [violence], and shutteth his eyes from seeing evil." This verse mentions two avenues to our minds— hearing violence and seeing evil. If we ever expect to stand in God's presence, these two avenues must be guarded.

Verse 16 is an assurance of God's care for us: "He shall dwell on high: his place of defence shall be the munitions of rocks: bread shall be given him; his waters shall be sure."

And the passage ends with the reward of faithfulness: "Thine eyes shall see the king in his beauty: they shall behold the land that is very far off."

In order to have moral principles, high values, and a burning zeal for the Lord, we must guard the avenues to our mind. Movies, television, and videos reach our minds primarily through the channels of our eyes. If you want to guard your mind from satanic influences through movies and television, you might want to consider the following:

1. You could decide to live without television or movies. Many do and are none the worse for it.

2. You could determine to be more selective in what you watch. If you must watch TV or videos, read the reviews and be more selective.

3. You could decide to spend at least as much time reading God's Word or other Christian literature as you do watching TV or movies.

The *Star Wars* trilogy introduced a fictional world in which humans fought against evil "spiritual forces." While this scenario was fictional, there is no fiction about the fact that a war between spiritual forces is being fought in the universe. There is a great controversy going on between Christ and the forces of good and Satan with his forces of evil. And we are not just idle spectators. The war is being fought over *us*. The mind and allegiance of every human on earth is the object of contention. Satan, as a roaring lion, is seeking to devour as many as he can, through whatever means it takes (see 1 Peter 5:8). He has rewrapped the lies with which he successfully deceived Eve in attractive new garb and is peddling them with phenomenal success to many unsuspecting and undiscerning Christians through the medium of movies. What we allow to enter our minds is of eternal consequence. We must wake up to the enemy's strategy before it is eternally too late.

Let's ask the Lord for a discerning spirit, and when error is placed before us in a tempting, enticing manner, ask the Lord to give us the courage to say No.

1. Caryl Matrisciana, *Gods of the New Age* (Eugene, Oreg.: Harvest House Publishers, 1985), 137.
2. Jovial Bob Stine, *Ghostbusters II Storybook* (New York: Scholastic, Inc., 1989).
3. A *conscious* channeler is a modern spirit medium who relays messages from a spirit entity to another person. A *trans*channeler allows the spirit entity to actually possess the body of the channeler. In the later case, the facial expression and the voice usually change to match the characteristics of the spirit entity.
4. *Religion in America*, 1990 report, 10.

CHAPTER

5

New Age Roots

It was a crisp Sunday evening in mid-March 1988. I was sitting in a classroom in a Texas college for a one-week intensive course, nervous and wondering if I had bitten off more than I could chew. After being out of school for almost twenty years, I was starting a D.Min. program in church administration. The class was a three-hour-credit course called Contemporary Trends, covering the religious trends in the world today.

One of the course requirements was a project paper, due some two months later. I decided on the topic "Reaching the Secular Mind With the Gospel." But something happened that changed not only the subject of my paper but opened up my eyes to a whole new world.

About a week after the class ended, I was back in southern California, where my family and I attended a camp meeting. That evening Will Baron, who had been in the New Age movement for twelve years and had even become a New Age priest, gave his conversion testimony. At that time he had not written the book for which he is now so well known, *Deceived by the New Age*. Nevertheless, I was impressed with his experience and intrigued by the subject. The following Monday I called my professor and told him I would like to change the subject of my paper to "The Subtle New Age Movement."

During the next two months I read several books on the New Age movement, mainly from a Christian perspective. The more I read, the more intriguing it became. It was like someone lifting a veil to reveal a picture I had never realized was there. It was like the pieces of a puzzle suddenly fitting together to make sense of things that had before seemed unrelated. I discovered that although I was somewhat acquainted with certain of these philosophies and beliefs, I had never identified them with the New Age movement until this time.

India and Hinduism

One of the books that I read with great interest was *Gods of the New Age*, written by Caryl Matrisciana, a naive but adventurous woman. Caryl had been raised in India, where her father had a business until India's independence from England. Then he felt it was time to return to England. But during those first thirteen years of her life, Caryl was exposed to the Indians' practice of Hinduism in their daily lives. At the time she had no particular interest in their beliefs. As a Catholic, she regarded them only as pagan customs. It wasn't until much later as an adult that she recalled and analyzed the practices she had observed in India and began to relate them to the New Age movement.

For instance, she had seen people on the street worshiping the sacred cows to the extent that some devotees would drink a mixture of cows' milk and urine. She knew of some Hindus who made cakes and presented them to cobras. She remembered seeing old Hindus practicing hatha yoga, not for physical fitness, but as a preparation for reincarnation—the cycle of life and death. In hatha yoga, the yogis practice control of "uncontrollable" body functions such as breathing and blood flow until they are actually able to slow them down. She remembered the philosophy that Hindus have regarding their poverty-stricken compatriots—beggars and the poor in this life are only receiving their due reward for the way they lived in their previous life. Therefore, there is very little sympathy shown for the myriads of beggars in India. Hindus believe that karma—the total sum of life's actions, good or bad, determines what a person will be in the next life. The possibilities range from being an insect (because of much bad karma) to returning again as a human.

The sixties

Upon returning with her family to England in the sixties, Caryl was immediately caught up in the countercultural youth revolution of drugs, free love, rock music, and the Age of Aquarius. It was the heyday of the Beatles, who were among the foremost in England and America to introduce to the Western world such Hindu beliefs and philosophies as reincarnation and the worship of Hindu gods and guru masters.

Singer George Harrison of the Beatles wrote the popular song, "My Sweet Lord," on the album *All Things Must Pass*. Its lyrics were deceiving. On the surface it appeared to be a Christian song with words such as, "I want to see my Lord." Thousands of Christians embraced the song. But the chorus distinctly revealed that it was a song dedicated to Krishna, one of the Hindu gods. There is no question as to what Harrison hoped to accomplish with his song. *Update Magazine* quoted him as saying,

> My idea in "My Sweet Lord," because it sounded like a "pop song," was to sneak up on them a bit. The point was to have the people not offended by "hallelujah" and by the time it gets to "Hare Krishna" they're already hooked, and their foot's tapping, and they're already singing along "hallelujah" to kind of lure them into a sense of false security. And then suddenly it turns into "Hare Krishna," and they will be singing that before they know what's happened.[1]

The sixties was the age of the beatniks and later the hippies, with their fascination for Zen Buddhism, especially its meditation aspects. It was the time of the Hare Krishna movement in America. Young people with their shaved heads, clad in orange robes, solicited and sold copies of the *Bhagavad-Gita* at airports and city street corners. This was the time of Woodstock in upper New York State.

It was the time of the musical *Jesus Christ Superstar* and *Hair*. Probably the most popular song that came out of the theatrical play *Hair* was the song entitled "This Is the Age of Aquarius." The song became the theme of the New Age movement and gave it its biggest boost among the hippies. In fact, *Hair* became a box-office success, selling out nearly everywhere it was performed. *Hair* was heavy, loud rock music. Thousands of young voices, swelling in harmony along with oscillating colored lights and sound effects, were all a part of the inescapable mass-mesmerizing atmosphere that converted thousands of young people to the new paradigm shift or the new cosmic consciousness.

At performances of *Hair*, young people were enticed with the forbidden taste of mind-altering drugs to "unlock the door" of their minds and "pull down the blinds" in order to gain total self-awareness.[2] "Let the sunshine in," sang the cast of *Hair*, while the audience responded, "Oh yes, oh yes, let the sunshine in."[3] In this euphoric state, many of the young people who went to see and hear *Hair* were converted to New Age thinking.

Caryl Matrisciana was one of those who was converted after attending *Hair*. She says, "*Hair* laid the foundation that prepared the world for the principles that underlie today's most influential mindset—New Age thinking."[4]

The seventies and eighties

In the seventies and eighties, the West was invaded with self-styled gurus, yogis, and swamis from the East, gaining disciples by the thousands, along with wealth and influence. Many young people chose a communal lifestyle that encouraged the free use of mind-altering drugs and liberalized sexuality. At this time, the New Age movement appealed primarily to high-school and college-age young people. The status-quo citizen found this form of New Age appalling and distasteful. Christians especially condemned this lifestyle.

But the eighties were different. The New Age took on a subtlety that has continued to this day. It became sophisticated, drawing into its movement such modern writers as John Naisbitt, the author of *Megatrends*—an analysis of the last two decades of this century and the trends to come after the year 2000. Theatrical stars Shirley MacLaine; Linda Evans; Sharon Gless from the TV drama, "Cagney and Lacey"; Oprah Winfrey; and singers John Denver and Dionne Warwick also joined the New Age ranks.

In the eighties, the floodgates of New Age books were opened; key among them was Marilyn Ferguson's book, *The Aquarian Conspiracy: Personal and Social Transformation in Our Time*, for which John Naisbitt wrote the Foreword. Ferguson's book is recognized to this day as the bible of the New Age in modern times. One of the first New Age bestsellers in the seventies was Richard Bach's *Jonathan Livingston Seagull*. It sold 10.8 million copies in a four-year period in the United States and over 25 million worldwide, sowing seeds of reincarnation in the minds of its readers. Richard Bach is a prolific New Age writer; you see his books even in airport bookstands. Today, practically every bookstore in the nation has a section marked New Age. Interestingly, many of these books have been dictated by "spirit entities," according to their authors.

One of these is author J. Z. Knight. This popular transchanneler has written many books dictated to her by Ramtha, "The Enlightened One"—a 3,500-year-old warrior from the mythological Atlantis. One book claims to have been dictated by an extraterrestrial from a UFO.

The eighties were also a time when the art of spirit mediums took on a revolutionary change from séances conducted in dark rooms by strangely dressed mediums to modern, clean, professional-looking New Age centers offering the services of many-degreed parapsychologists, clairvoyants, astrologers, and channelers. In the eighties channelers came out of the closet, and even professed Christians began openly channeling messages from spirit entities—for those who would pay a fee. J. Z. Knight, perhaps the best-known channeler and by far the wealthiest, is convinced that transchanneling for Ramtha is part of God's plan for her life. She feels "chosen to be the instrument of this magnificent and powerful teacher [Ramtha]."[5]

Medically speaking, the eighties were the right time for New Age holistic medicine to emerge. Medical and health care was being priced out of the reach of many working people. Doctors were swamped with more and more patients, leaving them less time for personal attention to individuals. And it was a time when people were concerned about good health and longevity. Alternative holistic health promised answers to all these problems—plus spiritual development.

Early American roots

But New Age roots go back farther than the sixties. They reach back to the 1800s, to the time of the transcendentalist movement in America, to American writers Henry David Thoreau and Ralph Waldo Emerson, who were among transcendentalism's leading lights and who were greatly influenced by Eastern philosophy.[6]

Modern spiritualism had its rebirth in the 1800s. On March 31, 1848, the Fox sisters heard rappings on the door of their Hydesville, New York, home.

Another movement that took place in the 1800s was the Theosophy movement, started by Madam Helena Petrovna Blavatsky (1831-1891). Blavatsky was an eccentric Russian noblewoman who came to America at the height of the spiritualist awakening. In 1875 she formed the Theosophical Society of America.[7]

This period was also the time of Charles Darwin and his celebrated findings embodied in *The Origin of Species*, which many occult circles appropriated for their own. Darwin's evolutionary theories fit perfectly with their notions of "gradual progress that was implicit in the emanationist cosmology of occultists and mystics, seeming to put the authority of science behind what they had already believed."[8]

The primary root

Tracing New Age roots a bit farther, we discover that they go back to Hinduism, Buddhism, Taoism—and even farther to Egypt and the ancient, Bible-condemned practices of astrology, clairvoyance, and communicating with the spirit world. Finally, we can trace the roots of these beliefs to the Garden of Eden, where we find the basic premise stated by the fallen angel of light himself, Lucifer. It's all recorded in Genesis 3. Eve wandered through the garden and came to the area where the forbidden tree was found. All of a sudden she found herself addressed by a beautiful serpent, a talking serpent, at that— Satan, the first channeler.

Channeling through the serpent, Satan engaged Eve in a conversation about God's instructions. She remembered them well, but the enemy said in essence, "God has not been candid with you, for you will not surely die. The truth is that God knows your eyes will be opened if you eat of this fruit. You'll become wise and be a god—as He is." In other words, "There is no death. People continue living forever, whether in the so-called life cycle of reincarnation or in the invisible spirit world." This is still the first tenet of the New Age movement. Satan's second lie was that humans can become gods. In fact, the New Age teaches that we *are* gods; therefore, we don't need God and can cast off His claims on our lives.

Is it any wonder New Age ideas are so appealing to people's desire for self-gratification and personal power? The New Age has no concept of sin, and therefore, no judgment. It offers wisdom and knowledge about the present and future. However, the appeal is only on the surface. Underneath is an appalling, hideous network—not of self-gratification, but of Satan-gratification and worship, as people discover when it's almost impossible to escape. We serve either Christ or the devil. "No man can serve two masters" (Matthew 6:24). "He that gathereth not with me scattereth," Jesus said (Matthew 12:30). Or as the apostle Paul put it: "Know ye not, that to whom ye yield yourselves servants to obey, his servants ye are to whom ye obey; whether of sin unto death, or of obedience unto righteousness?" (Romans 6:16).

What constitutes life and death?

The Bible teaches the truth about our human condition and what happens when we die. When God made Adam, He did not just call him into existence as He did the rest of the world. In this special act of creation, proposing to make man in His image, God used His hands and the elements He had already created to mold a man out of clay. Once He had formed Adam in an inanimate shape waiting to be energized with life, God breathed into Adam's nostrils the breath of life. Adam's breath was given to him by the only Source that gives life to the animate creatures in this world. It was a virtue of God that was instilled in Adam. The Bible records that when "God formed man of the dust of the ground," He "breathed into his nostrils the breath of life; and man became a living soul" (Genesis 2:7).

It was a combination of these two elements, the "dust of the ground" and the "breath of life," that made man a living soul, a living human being. It's simple chemistry—remove one from the other, and you have no living soul. "Then shall the dust return to the earth as it was: and the spirit [or breath] shall return unto God who gave it" (Ecclesiastes 12:7).

At the time of the Flood, as recorded in Genesis 7:21, 22, "All flesh died that moved upon the earth, both of fowl, and of cattle, and of beast, and of every creeping thing that creepeth upon the earth, and every man: all in whose nostrils was the breath of life, of all that was in the dry land, died."

There is no question that at the time of the Flood, everyone and everything that had the breath of life given by God died—with the exception of those in the ark. Where did this breath go? Just as the wise man said, it returned to God, who had given it at the beginning.

Solomon also said, "That which befalleth the sons of men befalleth beasts; even one thing befalleth them: as the one dieth, so dieth the other; yea, they have all one breath; so that a man hath no pre-eminence above a beast: for all is vanity" (Ecclesiastes 3:19). What do you think of that! God is the only One who can instill life. He is the only life-source for all living creatures. And when that breath of life is removed, men and animals alike are dead.

It works pretty much like the lamps and lights in your home. They are all in different rooms and in different locations of each room. They all have their own identity as far as where they are located. But once the switch is turned off, the electricity and the lamp are disconnected, and the light ceases to exist. That is why Solomon states:

> The living know that they shall die: but the dead know not any thing, neither have they any more a reward; for the memory of them is forgotten. Also their love, and their ha-tred, and their envy, is now perished; neither have they any more a portion for ever in any thing that is done under the sun. . . . [Therefore,] whatsoever thy hand findeth to do, do it with thy might; for there is no work, nor device, nor knowl-edge, nor wisdom, in the grave, whither thou goest (Ecclesiastes 9:5, 6, 10).

That's pretty straight and clear. What happens to the dead? Nothing. They are dead and remain in their graves, waiting to receive their eternal reward when Jesus comes the second time as King of kings and Lord of lords (see Revelation 17:14).

The New Testament teaches that the dead are awaiting the return of Christ. "Marvel not at this: for the hour is coming, in the which all that are in the graves shall hear his voice, and shall come forth; they that have done good, unto the resurrection of life; and they that have done evil, unto the resurrection of damnation" (John 5:28, 29).

The Bible truth is plain. There is only one life to live on this earth, not a continuous cycle of lives. We have only one opportunity to decide to live for Christ and serve Him. Or to choose to live for and serve the devil.

To many, the New Age movement may seem relatively harmless and innocent. What could be so wrong about seeking alternative New Age health treatments? Only that they are tied to occult philosophies and practices! What could be so wrong with possibility thinking? Only that possibility thinking, as defined by New Age ideas, leaves God out of the picture and considers Him to be a crutch for those who are weak and cannot pull themselves up by their own bootstraps. We Christians are success oriented all right, but in Christ. Paul says, "I can do all things through Christ which strengtheneth me" (Philippians 4:13). God has a definite plan for our lives and desires us to develop all our talents and gifts to their utmost for Him.

What could be so wrong in believing in reincarnation, sensing somehow that you lived in a different life? Only that it leads you to disregard Bible truth in regard to the true condition of the dead and the fact that you have only this life in which to decide for eternal life or eternal death.

The parable is told by Christ about the rich man and Lazarus (see Luke 16:19-31). Many miss the point of Jesus' parable, thinking it teaches that people are conscious after death and can communicate with the living. But that is not the point of Jesus' story at all. Far from it. The point Jesus was making is stated in the last two verses, in which the rich man pleads with Abraham to send someone from hell to his five brothers and warn them to change their ways and escape the torment he was experiencing.

Notice Abraham's response: "They have Moses and the prophets [the Bible]; let them hear them. . . . If they hear not Moses and the prophets, neither will they be persuaded, though one rose from the dead" (verses 29, 31). Jesus' point was that we have only this life in which to decide our eternal destiny and that the information upon which we can make that decision is found in God's Holy Word. We can never be led astray if we follow Bible truth.

No other god

The concept that human beings can become gods is foreign to the Bible; it is blatantly taken from paganism. The Bible teaches that we are God's creation and that we are to serve Him with our minds, our hearts, and souls. Paul states that there is only one God and one mediator between man and God, and that is Jesus Christ (see 1 Timothy 2:5). And the first commandment states it very clearly, "Thou shalt have no other gods before me" (Exodus 20:3).

God is the only true God; He says, "I am God, and there is none else" (Isaiah 45:22). We are not gods and never will be. Those who desire to be gods will end up as Lucifer did, desiring to be like the

Most High. And his fate will be theirs. "O Lucifer, son of the morning! how art thou cut down to the ground, which didst weaken the nations! For thou hast said in thine heart, I will ascend into heaven, I will exalt my throne above the stars of God: I will sit also upon the mount of the congregation, in the sides of the north: I will ascend above the heights of the clouds; I will be like the most High" (Isaiah 14:12-14).

Don't be deceived by the subtle New Age movement and those who have incredible testimonies regarding their experiences in any of its aspects.During the past decade, Satan has intensified his sophistries because he knows he has but a short time (see Revelation 12:12). Some of his deceptions come so close to the practice of truth that the unwary Christian may well be deceived. Be aware of that possibility as you read the next two chapters.

1. *Update Magazine*: 7 (December 1983), 23, as quoted in Norman L. Geisler and J. Yutaka Amano, *The Reincarnation Sensation* (Wheaton, Ill.: Tyndale House Publishers, Inc., 1986), 18.

2. Caryl Matrisciana, *Gods of the New Age* (Eugene, Oreg.: Harvest House Publishers, 1985), 11.

3. Ibid., 10, 11.

4. Ibid., 14.

5. J. Z. Knight, *A State of Mind, My Story: Ramtha: The Adventure Begins* (New York: Warner Books, 1987), 313.

6. Karen Hoyt, ed., *The New Age Rage* (Old Tappan, N.J.: Fleming H. Revell Company, 1978), 21.

7. Ibid., 23.

8. Ibid., 23, 24.

CHAPTER

6

Mystical and Christian Meditation—I

Are you into meditation? Have you tried its techniques as a means of dealing with your stress, tapping into your "inner" powers, or seeking a "closer" walk with God? Have you experimented with Transcendental Meditation (TM), yoga, or some other mystical form of meditation? If so, you are not alone.

Today meditation of every variety is widely accepted and practiced among millions of Americans on a regular basis.[1] In fact, meditation is so popular in the United States that you can find chapels for meditation in hospitals, airports, and even in our nation's legislative buildings. The United Nations has a meditation room, and the Pentagon has its own Meditation Club. Even among Christians, interest is so widespread that there are nearly two thousand Christian book titles on prayer, meditation, and techniques for spiritual growth.[2]

Although meditation has always been a legitimate part of Christianity, there appears to be a "meditation movement" in Christian circles today that incorporates New Age concepts and that is adversely affecting some sincere Christians. Take, for instance, Joey Orman, who was introduced to mystical meditation by a deacon in her church. He promised her "astro travel" and a closer walk with the Lord. But soon the cosmic energy forces she received overwhelmed her and caused a disorder in her central nervous system. Joey ended up in a psychiatric ward.

Some Christian leaders today are teaching, through seminars and books, questionable meditation techniques and such dangerous elements as "guided imagery" and "visualization." Christians are instructed to conjure up the image of Christ, dialogue with Him in their minds, and equate His messages (given through an "inner voice") with those of Scripture.

Satan has taken these mystical elements of Eastern religions and introduced them into Christian prayer and meditation to create a subtle, acceptable form of Christian discipline that is sweeping through the ranks of the church with alarming success.

Meditation in schools

Adults are not the only targets of New Age meditation teachings. At the same time Satan is passing off his candied apples as the golden fruit of meditation to adults, he is also unashamedly marketing these same wares to our children. Many are not aware that New Age meditation is being taught in the schools. Generally the term *meditation* is not used because of possible parental objection to their children learning such concepts. So it has been given a more neutral name such as *centering* or *focusing*, but the content is still the same. It's a mystical exercise of guided imagery and creative visualization. The process usually involves having the children sit or lie down and close their eyes. They are instructed to relax each muscle of their bodies, to lower their rate of breathing through breathing exercises, and finally to create mental scenes as their teacher describes them.[3]

Although these techniques are widely taught in many public schools, they have subtly crept into some Christian school curriculums as well. Christian teachers should be aware that there is an effort being launched to teach them New Age meditation concepts so that they in turn will educate their students in this new way of dealing with problems and stress. Those who are not aware of this hidden agenda may mistakenly teach concepts that are spiritually dangerous.

Some schools have a curriculum that includes "Rainbow for Relaxation," a program that supposedly helps children relax; it is essentially hypnosis.[4] The teacher guides the children's minds through the colors of the rainbow, telling them to rest their minds, feel calm, and move from one color to another. "Move down the rainbow and see the color purple. Begin to know the *real* you. Feel calm. Enter this *real* part of you." The children are told to repeat, "I like myself. I am happy. I have full control of myself. Every day, in every way, I am growing better, better, better." Then they are told that the more they practice this, the better they will get at it.[5]

The lesson that follows the rainbow relaxation exercise is called "Workshop and Helpers." This is where things begin to get really spooky. The teacher says:

> How would you like a special or custom-built house to go to anytime you want to, with anything you want in it? You could have any person you want to come and visit you. It wouldn't matter if he or she was dead or alive, real or imaginary. After today, you will always have this special place and special way of being with anyone you want. Be sure to use them.[6]

After the teacher leads the children through the building of their workshop or house, he or she says:

> Now sit down in your big chair behind your table and relax. Get ready to meet your two helpers. . . . First, you will see your male helper. He is behind the sliding door in your elevator. Use the control panel on the arm of your chair to make the door of your elevator open. . . . Now, look at your male helper. . . . He is now real and alive, and he comes into your workshop. . . . Say "Hello" and ask him his name . . . tell him how glad you are that he is there with you. Ask him either to sit or stand near you on your right side.[7]

Can you see where this is leading? God specifically tells us in Deuteronomy 18:10-12 that any attempt to contact the dead (necromancy) is an abomination to Him. He warns of grave consequences if we disregard His words. But your child may be being taught the methods of this abomination without even realizing it. And the fact that the child is introduced to the spirit in such an "innocent" way makes the danger all that much more subtle. The teacher tells the children that these "helpers" can teach, guide, listen to, and counsel them and that they will always be there on their right side whenever the child needs them. This is a blatant attempt to turn a Christian child from relying on the Bible for the answers to his problems. It even confiscates the trust that the child should have in relying on parents for answers. Imagine where this can lead children if they grow up relying on this friendly counsel for the solution to all their problems. It leads to the same place that visualization, TM, yoga, and guided imagery lead—into the twilight zone of modern-day spiritualism. A friend, with whom I shared this information, told me, "Now I'm beginning to understand what my preschool daughter was trying to tell me when she said she had been seeing Jesus at school. It was all so real to her."

Legitimate, biblical meditation is an excellent means of enhancing the spiritual life. However, many sincere Christians who desire a closer walk with Christ can be vulnerable to Satan's sophistry in the area of meditation if they are uninformed. Matthew 24:24 tells us that in the last days, Satan will work with such subtle deception that if it were possible he would deceive even the very elect. New Age meditation is one area in which he is most likely to be successful.

Why the interest in meditation?

Eastern mystics, especially Hindus and Buddhists, have practiced meditation (yoga) for centuries as a part of their religious, spiritual exercises. They also engage in "inner listening" or "inner communion." Hinduism's central goal is to escape physical rebirths (transmigration or reincarnation) and reach spiritual perfection—the nonphysical, spiritual, blissful state of nirvana, the ultimate reality. In order to reach this goal, Hindus alter their minds through meditation, hoping to gain wisdom, detach themselves from this physical world, unite themselves with Brahma (god), and finally to become gods themselves.

Westerners have picked up on aspects of these Eastern meditation practices for a variety of reasons. Some view it as a method to cope with stress. In a recent *Newsweek* article, Mary Talbot wrote that yoga is on the rise because stress is on the rise.[8] Others use meditation as a form of hypnotism to control undesirable habits. Still others enter mystical meditation with the hope of gaining esoteric or privileged information, as well as the power that comes from this knowledge.

Some Christians believe that Hindu meditation techniques such as hatha yoga are a practical way of handling daily stress, with the added bonus of increasing spirituality and intimacy with God. They claim that meditation helps them maintain mental, physical, and spiritual well-being. But perhaps the most prominent reason Christians become involved in meditation is for spiritual enrichment.

Almost without exception, wherever I have lectured on the dangers of New Age meditation, someone has approached me at the end of my presentation and said, "I know of someone in the church who talks with the Lord and receives messages from Him on a daily basis." Or "A seminar was given that taught meditation much as you describe New Age and Eastern meditation." These people go on to tell me about the importance that these Christian proponents of mystical meditation place on the *preparation* for meditation—rhythmic breathing, posture control, closing the eyes, guided imagery, the imaginary place where they are to meet the visualized "Christ," the actual dialogue with Him, and finally, keeping a careful journal of their experience. Most of these meditative practices have been extracted from Eastern religions and have been practiced by Hindus, Buddhists, shamans, gurus, and yogis for hundreds of years as part of their religious experiences.

Unfortunately, there are many well-meaning, but unsuspecting Christians who have ventured into practicing mystical meditation, believing it was "Christian" or at least compatible with their faith. To sincere Christians, meditation appears to be a way of attaining a higher level of spirituality, of achieving a more intimate communion with God. Through meditation, it appears that they have found a different way to intimacy with "Christ," a new way of putting life and meaning into their private devotional experience. But however beneficial it may appear to your health or spirituality, this meditation movement is dangerous and could lead down a path you will later regret. Self-induced visualization in meditation can be a potential hot line leading, not to God, but directly to the mind of Satan and his demons. God's people are not safe in trying to extract what they consider beneficial from the practices of pagan religions. Those religions are an abomination to the Lord.

When the Lord told King Saul to destroy the Amalekites and spare nothing, neither man, woman, nor beast, Saul thought he would save what was "good" (the best of the sheep and cattle) to sacrifice to the Lord. He took what he considered to be "good" from the pagans to use in his worship of the true God. And how did God respond to Saul's reasoning? He rejected Saul's reasoning; He rejected his sacrifices, his leadership, and finally rejected him.

What is biblical meditation?

Both Christian and Eastern meditation have been around for centuries. The question is: Are they one and the same? Similar? Compatible? Or grossly different? What is their purpose and function?

There is considerable confusion today regarding what is genuine biblical Christian meditation and what is not. It is often claimed that biblical meditation and Eastern meditation are parallel, or at times, one and the same. The truth is, philosophically, they are as far from each other as the east is from the west. The end result might well be the difference between eternal salvation and eternal damnation.

Part of the dilemma in distinguishing between biblical Christian meditation and Eastern or New Age meditation is that almost nowhere in the Bible is true Christian meditation fully described or elaborated on. The Scriptures mention only a few incidents alluding to meditation: Jesus going to a quiet place to pray in the morning while it was still dark (see Mark 1:35) or Isaac going out to meditate in the fields (see Genesis 24:63). Perhaps this lack of emphasis was intentional in order to prevent the practice of meditation from being structured into something that it should not be.

Basically, Bible writers used eight Hebrew words and two Greek words (see the listing in the appendix on pages 125 and 126) that are translated in the King James Version as "to meditate" or "meditation." In the Old Testament, the psalmist and other writers used the word *meditation* to refer to "contemplating, or thinking about" God's law (see Psalm 1:2). *Meditation* also was used to mean "the thoughts of one's heart, or mind" (see Psalms 19:14; 49:3).

From the way Scripture is generally understood, the phrase "meditating day and night" (see Joshua 1:8) seems to refer to an attitude of mind, not literally to sitting for twenty-four hours, quietly "meditating." When the apostle Paul admonished us to "pray without ceasing" (1 Thessalonians 5:17), he meant we should maintain a constant awareness of God, that we should always keep the communication lines of prayer open. So one biblical meaning of meditation is an attitude of mind—not something that is physically or mentally structured as a specific devotional ritual.

Other times, the Bible writers use the word *meditation* to refer to seeking a quiet place to contemplate or reflect on God (see

Psalm 64:6). Luke, in the New Testament, uses the word in the sense of thinking over a situation before answering or taking an action (see Luke 21:14). Another Bible use of the word *meditation* is found in Psalm 49:3 and refers to the utterance of one's heart. In general terms, the Bible uses *meditate* to mean "contemplate," focusing attention with our thoughts on a particular person or object in order to understand it more profoundly. Meditation is a normal intellectual process, something that is natural in our daily activities.

For Christians, meditation is usually done in connection with personal devotions while praying or prayerfully reading God's Word. Meditation requires no special bodily position or preparation. It involves concentrating on, or musing over, a passage, phrase, or word, asking God through His Holy Spirit to enlighten our minds regarding its relevance to our Christian experience. Meditation can also include filling our minds through our conscious imaginations with themes depicted or described in Scripture, such as God's great plan of salvation and immeasurable love for us; the second coming; or the life of Jesus, especially the closing scenes—His death on the cross, His resurrection from the tomb, and His ascension to heaven.

Christian meditation is not limited exclusively to biblical themes. It can involve any number of daily life experiences. Christian meditation may concern itself with major decisions presented to the Lord in prayer as we claim His promises for guidance and provision. It may be used in connection with seeking relief from, or gaining courage to face, a severe testing trial. We may meditate as we seek to understand God's will at some crucial time in our lives. There is no question but that Christian meditation is, and should be, an important part of the spiritual experience with our Creator and Saviour.

Our purpose for meditating should be to occupy or fill our minds with God's thoughts, to have the Holy Spirit illuminate our understanding or impress our minds regarding Scripture or biblically related experiences. Genuine biblical meditation is not a redeeming act or method of integration with one's higher self or with Hindu gods, as is Eastern meditation. Christians meditate in order to look outside themselves to God through Scripture and the Holy Spirit so that they may become more like Him in character.

On the other hand, Hindus, Buddhists, and shamans, who have

been practicing mystical meditation for many centuries, meditate for ultimately different reasons. Although some forms of Eastern meditation may appear outwardly to be harmless, they are definitely pagan and are foreign to Christianity.

Eastern meditation

Eastern meditation, in contrast to Christian meditation, requires that we attempt to empty the mind in preparation for meditation. It attempts to block out outside noises and still the senses in order to become in tune with the inner self.[9] Hindus, Buddhists, and others who practice introspective visualization meditation do so with the purpose of liberating themselves from the confines of present reality. When Christians meditate, they reach outside themselves to God; Eastern meditators attempt to go deep within the unconscious state of their own minds to discover their superconsciousness, their higher self, and ultimately to integrate themselves with universal spirits or entities. For the Hindu, reaching this goal is Brahma—the ultimate reality or god-consciousness. By uniting with the mind of their god(s), they believe they can become gods themselves.

This concept is also espoused by the New Agers. For example, Shirley MacLaine, a leading New Age proponent, gives her view of meditation:

> The object of meditation is to conduct a dialogue with the highest source of our faculties and hence tie in to the universal sources of strength. Calming the body and the mind helps us to connect to the answers that await our questions.[10]

MacLaine doesn't mention a personal God, but notice the phrase "universal sources of strength," which is very similar to the Eastern religious views of a "universal consciousness."

Eastern meditation is done in three phases: (1) relaxation, (2) interiorization, and (3) expansion. Let's take a look at an actual meditation ritual of Eastern religions as outlined in John Novak's book, *How to Meditate*.

The process, stated simply, is:

Phase I   Relax completely, both physically and mentally.

Phase II   Interiorize the mind and concentrate it pointedly on one's own higher self or some aspect of God.

Phase III Expand one's consciousness until his individual mind merges with the infinite.[11]

Physical positions—relaxation

Eastern meditators take very seriously the preparation for meditation and physical positions. They begin by relaxing their bodies and minds. They seek out a quiet place, where they sit down, usually in what the Hindus call the "lotus" position. The lotus position involves sitting cross-legged on the floor with torso held upright and eyes closed. This position is the most common meditative posture used in Eastern countries and is regarded as facilitating communion with the spirits.

When Hindus sit in a lotus position to meditate, they position themselves for the unwinding of the dormant *kundalinī* (the "serpent power" at the base of the spine). This position makes it possible for the *kundalinī* to pass up through the spine and activate the seven "chakras," the mystical nerve centers that they believe are located in the upper torso and head. One of the most powerful of these chakras, they teach, is the heart chakra, supposedly located in the area of the human heart. The sixth chakra, or the third eye, is located between the eyebrows; the seventh is the crown chakra on top of the head.

The lotus position is named after the flower of that name which looks similar to a yellow rose. It is the national flower of India and has been considered sacred in Egypt, India, and China. But the lotus is more than just a pretty flower; it has spiritual significance. For the Hindu, the opening of the lotus petals symbolically represents the opening of the fourth, or heart, chakra, to receive spirits or mystical energies of the cosmic realms. So employing this position for meditation carries pagan spiritual implications.

Some Christians may reason that all these ideas are simply foolish notions and therefore harmless. But when a person engages in a practice that is pagan, Satan is all too willing to display his power through these mystical entryways.

Easterners also meditate in the "corpse" position (*asvasana*) in which, as the name suggests, the body is stretched out on the floor. In the West, the *asvasana lyind* corpse position is often used when teaching meditation to children. In yet another position, yogis sit erect on a straight-backed chair. They concentrate deeply and are very methodical in their breathing, inhaling and exhaling in a rhythmic manner in order to enter the first phase of relaxation and subsequent altered state of consciousness. The chair position is the one most commonly used by New Agers in Western countries.

Eastern meditation also places much importance on the position of the hands. The hands generally rest on the knees or thighs, with the palms turned upward, cupped as receptacles to receive cosmic spiritual energies and impulses.

Mantras—for concentration

Mantras, or incantations, are words or short phrases taken from the Hindu Sanskrit scriptures and are believed to possess supernatural powers when repeated in a chant.[12] When properly said, they resonate through the nasal system, enhancing the preparation for meditation. Mantras are given to a meditator by his yoga, or meditation, leader. Some are very private and are known only to their owner, while others are common for anyone to use. Probably the most common and popular of the resonating types is the "Om."

Another common mantra is "amen." Upon inhaling, the meditator softly says "a"; upon exhaling he says "men." Some mantras are blatantly blasphemous, such as "I am He." It is broken into two phrases: as the individual breathes in, he says "I am . . ." As he exhales, he says ". . . He." What he is really saying is, "I am God." Shirley MacLaine, while doing her hatha yoga, poses and meditates, chanting: "I am God in Light."[13]

In typical Western New Age meditation, mantras are optional and often are not used at all.

Listening—hearing the voice of God

In New Age–style Eastern meditation, the mechanisms of physical relaxation; posture control; deep, rhythmic breathing; and efforts to quiet the mind are all preparatory steps leading to the activity of "listening." This listening is not a process of using the physical ears, but is rather an activity of listening to "inner messages" perceived in the mind. This is sometimes known as listening to an "inner voice." In his book *Deceived by the New Age*, former New Age priest Will Baron describes the meditation "listening" process as taught to him by his leader, Muriel (leader of the Lighted Way metaphysical center):

"Don't search for a voice that you can hear audibly with your ears. . . . It isn't like that. The higher self speaks through your mind as you attune to it. Now at other times, God can speak to us through his emissaries, the masters. But again, the masters will use the vehicle of your higher self in order to communicate with you. They speak through your conscience. With practice, you will be able to identify what comes from the higher realms."[14]

Yogis, while meditating, listen to the "inner voice" of their higher self or their spirit masters (among which they include Christ), similar to the listening process followed by New Agers as described above.

Among Christians, the Quakers, or the Society of Friends, have historically been the religious group that has stressed the need to enter into "the listening silences"[15] as they refer to listening to the voice of God. Quakers believe that the worship of God is the primary purpose of religious life. But unlike the traditional forms of worship used by other Christians, Friends worship in silence. At the appointed time, without prearrangement, they wait in silence for the flow of "spiritual messages, vocal prayer, Bible reading, or ministry—from anyone who feels called to participate."[16]

Richard J. Foster, a Quaker, describes Christian meditation as simply the "ability to hear God's voice and obey his word." He quotes Dietrich Bonhoffer to explain this notion: "Just as you do not analyze the words of someone you love, but accept them as they are said to you, accept the Word of Scripture and ponder it in your heart as Mary did. That is all. That is meditation."[17]

Visualization—expanding consciousness

Visualization is the second phase of Eastern meditation and can be described as "introspection," going within to contact and sense your higher self, the "god" within you. It is using your imagination to create reality. Hindu yogis, who are among the most devoted meditators, avidly practice what in the West is referred to as creative visualization and imagery techniques.

Visualization is not the same as using the imagination in Christian mediation to contemplate the life of Jesus or to picture in the mind the great spiritual themes of Scripture. The aim of Eastern introspective meditation is to bypass the reasoning areas of the brain and go deep into the mind to contact one's "higher self" or "higher consciousness." It endeavors to put the individual in touch not only with the so-called divine powers within, but also with the spirit entities of the universe that give guidance and counsel. Christian New Agers claim that God "often appears to saints in this manner" and that "by visualizing an expansive scene we build a bridge from individual to universal consciousness."[18] The results can be obtaining mystical powers, "out-of-body experiences," the spirit leaving the physical body, or visualizing "spirit guides" and receiving counsel from them.

Christians believe that man's nature is basically sinful. "All have sinned, and come short of the glory of God" (Romans 3:23). Christians believe that we are saved by grace through faith, and not of ourselves (see Ephesians 2:8). Neither God nor grace are to be found by looking inward to our own self. We are to look outside ourselves for salvation. We are to deny self, not make it into a god. The philosophy that there is inherent wisdom and godhood within us originated with Satan in the Garden of Eden and is perpetuated by New Age "Christian" writers such as M. Scott Peck in his bestseller, *The Road Less Traveled*: "If you want to know the closest place to look for grace," Peck says, "it is within yourself. If you desire wisdom greater than your own, you can find it inside you."[19] This is New Age teaching, totally opposed to Christianity. Yet I attended a Christian church in which Peck's book was the textbook being discussed during that quarter. Is it any wonder that people are confused about what is truth and what isn't? God help us to get back to the Bible!

1. John J. Novak, *How to Meditate* (Nevada City, Calif.: Crystal Clarity Publishers, 1989), 13.
2. "Religion: Talking to God," *Newsweek*, 6 January 1992, 40.
3. Eric Buehrer, *The New Age Masquerade* (Brentwood, Tenn.: Wolgemuth & Hyatt Publishers, Inc., 1990), 89.
4. Ibid., 96.
5. Ibid., 97.
6. Ibid., 98.
7. Ibid., 99.
8. "Om Is Where the Heart Is," *Newsweek*, 3 February 1992.
9. Bob Larson, *Straight Answers on the New Age* (Nashville, Tenn.: Thomas Nelson Publishers, 1989), 52.
10. Shirley MacLaine, *Going Within: A Guide for Inner Transformation* (New York: Bantam Books, 1989), 75.

11. Novak, *How to Meditate*, 11.
12. Larson, *Straight Answers on the New Age*, 114.
13. MacLaine, *Going Within*, 68.
14. Will Baron, *Deceived by the New Age* (Boise, Idaho: Pacific Press Publishing Association, 1990), 39.
15. Richard J. Foster, *Celebration of Discipline* (San Francisco: Harper & Row, 1988), 22.
16. Leo Rosten, *A Guide to the Religions of America* (New York: Simon and Schuster, Inc., 1955), 124.
17. Richard J. Foster, *Celebration of Discipline*, 17, 29.
18. Novak, *How to Meditate*, 52.
19. M. Scott Peck, M.D., *The Road Less Traveled* (New York: Simon and Schuster, 1978), 281.

CHAPTER

7

Mystical and Christian Meditation—II

In the previous chapter we saw that mystical meditation techniques and practices are being taught and practiced by Christians. Many are unaware of the background of these ideas or their implications. Unsuspecting Christians need to be warned of the subtle dangers inherent with meditation techniques that incorporate aspects of visualization; they need to be shown where these things can lead.

It is true that biblical meditation has not always been well defined or even, until recently, been a topic of Christian writers. As a result, well-intended people have experimented with forms of New Age or Eastern meditation; some have even attempted to "baptize" it and call it Christian meditation. The danger is subtle, yet deadly. The counterfeit is close to the genuine, but it is dangerous and forbidden ground for Christians.

One of the more prevalent practices in New Age meditation is guided imagery and subsequent visualization.

In guided imagery, one person verbally guides another person into using his or her imagination to create specific images. Visualization is based on the concept that thoughts can create reality. The spirit entity that most Christians seek to contact through visualization is, not surprisingly, Christ.

Christian pastor and author C. S. Lovett, in his book *Longing*, writes:

> Turn on your imagination screen. . . .We're going to do an

EXERCISE that can help you visualize the Lord. I want to make sure you have a clear mental picture of Him.[1]

To aid you in your visualization of "Christ," these Christian teachers of meditation guide you step by step through a mental process of visualization. You are first taken through a relaxation exercise. Then you are encouraged to visualize, or form a mental image, of some special place such as a tranquil garden, a sandy beach, or a private study. It can be an actual place you know or just make-believe. But you are told to create your own unique, special place—your favorite kind of day, a peaceful, relaxing situation. This is the place in your mind to which you can always retire whenever you desire to meditate or perhaps to simply escape the pressures of life.

When you are comfortably situated in your meditation retreat, your teacher tells you to picture the face and form of Christ. You are then told that He is coming to meet with you. If you are at home, He stops at the door and knocks. You open the door, and "Christ" is standing there waiting to be asked in. Of course, you ask Him in, seat Him at the special place you have created in your mind, and then actually engage in a two-way conversation with "Jesus." You ask Him anything you want and listen to His voice as He answers you. Then He says He must leave but promises to meet with you again whenever you need Him.

This practice is insidiously dangerous because of its subtle appeal to Christians. What Christian wouldn't want to have an audience with Christ, to ask Him the difficult and unanswerable questions of life? And what more acceptable way of approaching Him than through meditation?

Commenting on this practice, Dave Hunt and T. A. McMahon, in their book *The Seduction of Christianity* warn:

> To create a fantasy of Jesus in our minds and insist that this is the *real* Jesus and that talking with this figment of our imagination is the way to genuine spiritual experience is to be deluded indeed. . . . In any such techniques, the definite possibility exists of opening the door to demonic contact or even of acquiring a "spirit guide" that we think is the real Jesus.[2]

Johanna Michaelsen, in her book *The Beautiful Side of Evil*, describes her involvement with a seminar on mind control in which her teacher used this guided imagery method to teach her how to attain a state of altered consciousness where she could meet her spiritual counselor.

She was first instructed to create a laboratory of her own choosing that was to be her haven and refuge, a place for solving problems. This laboratory could appear any way she chose. Johanna imagined a cave with walls of amethyst and emerald crystals and a shimmering golden light glowing from within. She was instructed to furnish her imaginary room with items such as filing cabinets for problems and a chair, which she imagined as a large blue velvet armchair in front of the fireplace. When told to choose her counselors, anyone from "Buddha to Grandma Moses," she had no question in her mind whom she would select. There was no higher source of wisdom than Jesus, she believed, so she chose Him. At first she thought this might be a presumptuous request, but then she remembered His words, "Behold, I stand at the door, and knock: if any man hear my voice, and open the door, I will come in to him" (Revelation 3:20).

The first time "Jesus" appeared to her, he was loving and gentle, with a glowing light around him. The second time he appeared, however, he had a horrible-looking face like a werewolf with blood all over its fur. At other times he would change from a werewolf to Jesus and back again. This, he explained, was to teach her not to be afraid of anything ugly. "Beneath the ugly," he told her, "there is always something beautiful."

Christians should resist any attempt of someone to control their thoughts and guide them into this dangerous form of meditation.

The Garden Meditation ritual

New Age advocates of meditation have attempted to disguise Eastern meditation practices by cloaking them in Christian terminology and by using Christ as the "spirit guide" who meets the Christian during his meditation practices. Notice how elements of Eastern meditation and Christian concepts are incorporated into the following Garden Meditation ritual as taught by The Lighted Way, a "Christian" New Age center. Here are the meditation instructions, as given in one of this group's publications:[3]

1. See your body, emotions and mind filled with the golden light of Christ. This means that you will be sitting in a golden sun. The gold light will be radiating about thirty inches from your physical form.

2. AFFIRM: "I am a child of God and I am returning home to the Father's house upon a path of light I call 'The Lighted Way.' "

3. Enter into your garden. Look at the trees, flowers and lake that you have. This is the space God created for you. Enjoy your space!

4. Invite Jesus Christ into your garden. He is your protector from lesser entities.

5. Sit under your tree of eternal life, light, and immortality. You may select a fruit from the tree to eat.

6. Talk to Jesus. Speak to Him of your needs; ask Him anything your heart desires.

7. Listen to Jesus. He will talk with you. This is the very beginning of a relationship with Christ that will take you into immortality.

8. Close with a prayer to the Father. "Father, I am your child. My name was written in the Book of Life before the foundations of the world were laid." Tell the Father your needs. God fulfills all promises. "Thank You, Father, in Jesus' name."

9. Spread the light from your garden to your home, work, the Lighted Way, anywhere or place or person whom you choose to receive the Christ Light. Then spread the light around the whole world as a blessing to the planet and humanity.

Note that these instructions subtly weave in biblical allusions that would be familiar to Christians. Jesus is associated with a golden light because light has always been used to manifest the presence of God—for example, the Shekinah, the pillar of fire, and the light that appeared to Saul on the way to Damascus. But there are some major points of conflict with the Bible as well. The instructions seem to indicate that Christians can create a "tree of life" in the mind and that it is permissible to eat the fruit from it. Bear in mind, too, that it is one thing to imagine that you see Jesus. It is another thing to actually engage in conversation with Him through your imagination. However, in the altered state of consciousness into which this exercise takes a person, he or she is no longer in control of the conscious faculties; anyone and anything has access to the mind, even Satan himself.

If by chance you are practicing meditation techniques that bear any similarity to the New Age meditation described above, you are on dangerous ground.

Dangers of visualization and guided imagery

Let's look at several inherent dangers of those kinds of meditation that involve a self-imposed trance state, visualization, or guided imagery.

1. Such meditation can open the mind's door to demonic influence and subsequent communication with Satan's angels.

Some Christian leaders who teach mystical meditation will ask their students to imagine a person who reminds them of Christ, someone who had a part in their spiritual growth—including persons no longer alive. The student is asked to create the image of that person in his or her mind. If that someone who was spiritually helpful to you happens to be your deceased mother, and she begins to speak to you, would you accept it as reality? Knowing that the Bible tells us the dead know nothing (see Ecclesiastes 9:5, 6), you would have to conclude that an evil spirit was talking to you.

By sustaining such a mental picture, unsuspecting or curious Christians can inadvertently alter their conscious states and unlock the door of the mind to the supernatural world. T. E. Wade, in his book *Spirit Possession: The Counterfeit With Many Faces*, states that seeking spiritual growth by any means of altered consciousness while meditating leads to contact with supernatural evil forces. Even without specific invitation, these supernatural forces can contact those who practice them.[4]

2. We can be deceived regarding Christ's coming.

Christ tells us that just before His return, "There shall arise false Christs, and false prophets, and shall shew great signs and wonders; insomuch that, if it were possible, they shall deceive the very elect" (Matthew 24:24). In verse 26 He continues, "Wherefore if they shall say unto you, Behold, he is in the desert; go not forth: behold, he is in the secret chambers; believe it not." Could this text perhaps apply to visualization in meditation? Even if you have actually visualized Jesus in the "secret chambers" of your mind, believe it not. Christ has warned us that it is a false "Christ" who will appear in the chambers, and He says that those who do not heed the warning will be deceived.

3. *We may be led to presumptuous or even blasphemous acts against Christ and the Holy Spirit.*

The Bible says nothing about visualizing or "creating" Jesus Christ in order to converse with Him. There is no reference to anyone purposely doing this. Instead, the Bible focuses on communication with God through prayer, His Word, and the influence of the Holy Spirit. Biblical characters who saw Christ, other than those who were contemporaries with Him, did so as a result of a vision initiated by heaven and not by them. When we visualize "Christ," it may very well be a demonic spirit.

> Scripture demonstrates that God has always taken the initiative when supernatural communication with man was necessary. Visions and dreams were given to His agents when God saw fit.[5]

Jesus did not teach His disciples to conjure Him up in a meditative vision after He returned to heaven. His words of comfort to them were: "I will pray the Father, and he shall give you another Comforter [the Holy Spirit], that he may abide with you for ever; even the Spirit of truth; whom the world cannot receive, because it seeth him not, neither knoweth him: but ye know him; for he dwelleth with you, and shall be in you" (John 14:16, 17). It is the Holy Spirit's work to teach us "all things" and to bring all things to our remembrance, even the instructions of Christ (see verse 26). It is the Holy Spirit's responsibility to guide us into all truth (see John 16:13). Christ did not say, "Visualize Me, and I'll come and teach you all things." He did, however, promise to be with us through His representative, the Holy Spirit.

When Jesus appeared to His disciples in the upper room after

His resurrection, Thomas was not present and therefore did not see Him for another week. Yet Thomas did not try to envision Jesus in His mind in order to talk with Him and see the evidence the others had seen. Instead, when Jesus saw Thomas, He said, "Blessed are they that have not seen, and yet have believed" (John 20:29). It is not sight we are told to seek, but faith in the unseen.

God is always available to us through prayer, but do we have a right to conjure Him up at our own will and time? Can we cause Him to "appear," in essence "creating" our Creator at our wish? This is unbiblical and blasphemous. By employing this method we force Christ into the mold of a cosmic genie or a crystal-ball spirit to wait on us at our command. This is demeaning to Christ and presumptuous on our part.

4. There is a tendency for those who teach "mystical Christian meditation" to equate the counsel they receive from their visualized images with biblical truth.

This is a very dangerous application to make. For example, suppose "the Christ" that you meet in your meditation instructs you to do something slightly different from (or even opposed to) the instructions in the Bible? Which would you follow? What if He should tell you that because of your particular situation, you are exempt from keeping one of the commandments, that in your case, an affair would not be considered adultery? Would that justify you to act contrary to God's Word?

5. Meditation can eventually supplant Bible study and prayer.

If you are visualizing Jesus, having one-to-one counseling sessions with Him, asking Him any questions you want and receiving His answers, why would you need the Bible anymore? Jesus could audibly answer any question you might have.

In time, this type of mystical, imaginary meditation could well become more meaningful than any other aspect of your devotional life. It could supplant personal Bible study and prayer. Why would you want to study and think about a difficult passage in Scripture if you could ask Christ directly for understanding? Or why would you want to pray day after day about a serious situation, waiting for the answer through God's providence, if you could bypass all that and get a concise answer in meditation?

6. The focus of your life can eventually turn inward.

If the answers to all life's problems can be answered by "Christ" through meditation, the tendency would be to eventually withdraw inside oneself. This is the opposite of Christ's command to go to all the world preaching the gospel. Instead of trying to find fulfillment inside ourselves, Christ tells us to be concerned for others. Meditation should not become an escape from the world, but a time to reflect on God's law.

God does impress our minds with His thoughts, and occasionally you may hear His voice saying, "This is the way, walk ye in it" (Isaiah 30:21). Certainly such Bible characters as Elijah (see 1 Kings 19:9), Isaiah (see Isaiah 6:8), and Peter (see Acts 10:13) received direct counsel from God. But this kind of communication is initiated by God, not by us. The truth is, the Jesus you visualize in mystical meditation reflects only *your* imagination, not God's thoughts.

> When miserable men do seek after God . . . they do not conceive of him in the character in which he is manifested, but imagine him to be whatever their own rashness has devised. . . . With such an idea of God, nothing which they may attempt to offer in the way of worship or obedience can have any value in his sight, because it is not him they worship, but, instead of him, the dream and figment of their own heart."[6]

God has left us with sufficient means to know His will and communicate with Him. First, we have the Scriptures. In Jesus' parable of the rich man and Lazarus, the rich man asked Father Abraham to send one from the dead to warn his five brothers of the suffering he was going through so they would believe. But Abraham answered by saying, "They have the Scriptures. If Scripture cannot convince them, neither will they be persuaded by one coming from the dead" (see Luke 16:28-31). God's written Word was sufficient.

Second, we have the Comforter, the Holy Spirit, to guide us and lead us to all truth. Jesus admonished us to pray for the Holy Spirit, not Himself, to come to us.

Third, we have prayer and true, biblical meditation to concentrate our minds on His Word and elevate our thoughts to heaven.

Fourth, we have faith, without which it is impossible to please God (see Hebrews 11:6), to enable us to accept the things we can't fully understand. Part of the sanctification process is to develop full confidence in God's leading in our lives.

Conjuring up a "Christ" and trusting implicitly in his counsel can short-circuit all of these avenues that God has given us to understand His will.

Transcendental meditation

This popular form of meditation is practiced on two levels: as a relaxation technique and as a means of "contributing solutions to all basic areas of human problems."[7] In transcendental meditation, *transcendental* means to transcend or go beyond the usual limits of knowledge, to go beyond nature into the supernatural. In transcendental meditation, a person tries to rise above distractions and focus on nothing in order to clear his mind; he attempts to achieve god-consciousness.

It might be well to examine the roots of this spurious form of meditation that is becoming so prevalent in Christian churches today. If we know its origins, it may help us to be more discerning of its deceptive practices.

Transcendental meditation (TM) is a modern form of Eastern or pagan meditation introduced to the West by Maharishi Mahesh Yogi in 1959. The Maharishi, or "Great Seer," claims that TM's roots go back thousands of years to Krishna, the fabled founder of Hinduism. U.S. college campuses were the first to open their doors to the Maharishi; he lectured and founded a student TM organization called the Students' International Meditation Society (SIMS). The students' interest in TM was phenomenal. Within six years "SIMS claimed to have more than 10,000 members in the U.S."[8] Before long, both public and private high schools began offering adult education classes in transcendental meditation. The YMCAs got into the act as well.

In his lectures, Maharishi Yogi claimed that TM was nothing more than a scientific technique that could relieve stress and lower blood pressure, along with providing other benefits such as increased sexual performance. However, even though he was emphatic about the fact that TM was not a religion or a religious technique, its practices demonstrated otherwise.

A prospective meditator had to undergo an initiation ceremony for which he must remove his shoes before entering a candle-lighted, incense-filled room. There he had to place a flower offering on a new, clean, white handkerchief in front of a picture of Guru Dev. All the while an initiator would sing a "puja" hymn and bow and kneel before the picture of Dev, instructing the initiate to do the same. The purpose of this initiation was to give the new meditator his mantra, a secret word essential for the practice of TM.[9]

A Christian would have some serious scruples against complying with such initiation requirements, as they demand breaking the first two of the Ten Commandments.

Psychology Today describes transcendental meditation as "clearly a revival of ancient Indian Brahmanism and Hinduism whose origins lie in the ancient text—Vedas, Upanishads, and Bhagavad-Gita; the teachings of the Buddha."[10]

Yoga

Yoga is not fully understood in the West. To most Western minds, yoga is a means of obtaining physical fitness. Many may not realize that "yogas" are spiritual disciplines in the Hindu's religious life. In Christian terminology, we might say that they are ways of sanctification for Hindus. The origins of yoga go back thousands of years and are rather obscure. Justin O'Brien, in his book *Christianity and Yoga: a Meeting of Mystic Paths*, states that yoga is a

systematic science, a set of techniques, and while yoga itself is not a religion, its practical teachings are an integral part of the great religions of the world. . . . Its central teaching is that man's essential nature is divine, perfect and infinite. . . .Through the meditative methods of yoga one can dispel the darkness of ignorance, and become aware of his essential nature, which is free from all imperfections.[11]

The word *yoga* in Hindi means "union," and yogis in India practice it to seek a union with their gods. Hatha yoga is a spiritual discipline designed to integrate the practitioner with his or her "higher self" and also with the spirit entities. Hatha yoga also is a means of manipulating bodily functions not normally under conscious control—breathing, blood flow, and metabolism. Some become so advanced in this spiritual art of meditation that they can stop their breathing for long periods. Hatha yoga is a preliminary meditation for four more spiritually advanced forms of yoga. These four higher yogas are also called "the four paths to god." They are: bhakti yoga (to god through love), jnana yoga (to god through knowledge), karma yoga (to god through work), and raja yoga (to god through meditative exercises).[12]

Yoga and transcendental meditation are based on Hindu beliefs and practices. The ultimate goal for advanced yogis is to attain union with Brahma, the all-pervading universal spirit, the Hindu concept of the cosmic god. Devout Hindus endeavor to eliminate all activity, both physical and mental, submitting to the universal spirit, Brahma, in order to integrate themselves with the mind of the cosmic god.

Although Westerners who practice yoga may not share this goal, they are participating in pagan religious exercises, and these practices can eventually lead them farther into Hindu practices of visioning and spiritualism. The Himalayan International Institute of Yoga Science and Philosophy in Honesdale, Pennsylvania, is a study center where yoga and meditation are taught for the betterment of society. How do those in this organization see their role? "They view the institute as 'building a bridge between the perennial truths of the East and the modern discoveries of the West.' "[13]

The most popular yoga in the West is hatha yoga, which involves physical postures and meditation, including the popular "lotus" position for meditating. Hatha yoga is presented as beneficial for one's mental and physical well-being, without exposing its occult roots and pagan religious significance.

In some of the yoga concepts one may see a slight similarity to Christian concepts, but on looking deeper beneath the surface, it becomes clear that they are totally different. The Hindus worship many "gods," whereas Christians worship the one Creator God. Hinduism has no concept of sin, judgment, or death—only karma, transmigration/reincarnation, and nirvana. Christians believe not only in sin and a judgment, but in Jesus as their Saviour from sin and their righteous Judge. The Hindu belief regarding death and reincarnation is the opposite of what Christians believe about life, death, and resurrection.

Nonetheless, under the guise of a physical fitness program, hatha yoga is offered in many urban centers in such places as YMCAs, college physical-fitness curriculums, and even Christian churches.

Is this an activity in which Christians should participate? Should we have anything to do with practices that are a part of a pagan religion or its philosophy? Are we able to ascertain what might be "good" or "beneficial" and extract it from its pagan origins without incurring God's displeasure? We should sincerely examine our meditation practices to discover where the roots lie. Then we may ask ourselves: Are we eating from the tree of the knowledge of good and evil while expecting its fruit to bring us the benefits of the tree of life?

1. C. S. Lovett, *Longing to Be Loved* (Baldwin Park, Calif.: Personal Christianity, 1982), 88.
2. Dave Hunt and T. A. McMahon, *The Seduction of Christianity: Spiritual Discernment in the Last Days* (Eugene, Oreg.: Harvest House Publishers, 1987), 163.
3. Unpublished materials copyrighted by Muriel Isis, *The Lighted Way*, Pacific Palisades, California.
4. T. E. Wade, *Spirit Possession: The Counterfeit With Many Faces* (Auburn, Calif.: Gazelle Publications, 1990), 75.
5. T. E. Wade, *Spirit Possession*, 77.
6. Hunt and McMahon, *The Seduction of Christianity*, 165.
7. Keith A. Gerberding, *How to Respond to Transcendental Meditation* (St. Louis: Concordia Publishing House, 1977), 12.
8. David Sneed and Sharon Sneed, *The Hidden Agenda* (Nashville, Tenn.: Thomas Nelson Publishers, 1991), 136.
9. Sneed and Sneed, *The Hidden Agenda*, 138.
10. *Psychology Today*, April 1974, 38.
11. Justin O'Brien, *Christianity and Yoga: a Meeting of Mystic Paths* (London: Arkana, 1989), xi.
12. J. Gordon Melton, ed., *The Encyclopedia of American Religions*, 3rd ed., 161, 162.
13. Sneed and Sneed, *The Hidden Agenda*, 141.

8

New Age Potpourri

In this chapter we will look at how New Age influences have entered into our everyday lives through a variety of avenues.

New Age music

One day, driving home in the evening rush hour of Los Angeles, I turned on the radio to find some easy-listening music. I scanned the dial until I came across a station playing soothing, relaxing music. It appealed to me. Here I was, stuck in four o'clock traffic, stressed out and anxious to get home. The music on this station seemed to hit the spot. I must have listened to it for about an hour until I arrived home.

Later, I did a little research into this station with its new sound. I discovered it was a New Age music station playing only New Age music, designed not only to unwind you after a hard day at the office but also to help prepare you for New Age meditation. One listener commented that listening to this music was "like I tapped into a radio station on Mars."[1] New Age radio stations are springing up throughout the nation. Even the Grammy Awards recognize New Age music. As of 1987 the awards now include this category.

Sometimes when I mention New Age music to people, what comes to their minds is rock or heavy-metal music. But New Age music is far from being rock. Indeed, some light and heavy rock music promotes certain New Age beliefs. However, New Age music usually involves relaxing sounds intended to affect the consciousness and specifically to cause the listener to relax. It appeals to

educated people with jobs that are exciting or mentally compli-
cated. The music helps them unwind. However, the melody or tune
is such that it is difficult to recall or hum after it is turned off.

Some New Age music is intended to do more than relax you.
Meditative or mystical New Age music is designed to be mind
altering, to prepare a person to enter meditation. This kind of
music is instrumental, with no lyrics, such as Steven Halpern's
"Spectrum Suite." This piece was specifically written to enable its
listeners to concentrate on the seven energy centers of their body
("chakras" in Eastern mystical belief).[2] New Agers call it "mind-
trip" music. Andrea Vollenweider, a Swiss harpist, believes that
New Age music can help build a bridge between the conscious and
subconscious mind.

Some artists reveal the intent of their music on the album covers
or through the title: "The Eternal Om" and "Journey Out of the
Body." Advertising may label it "inner harmony New Age music."
Some of this music may contain subliminal messages designed to
alter your thoughts.[3]

Another type is "progressive New Age music." It is mellow, but
uses instruments to stimulate. An example is the theme from the
movie "Chariots of Fire." Another category is called "Christian New
Age Music." These songs combine light jazz, folk, rock, and classical
music and may even be variations on hymns and choruses.

Caution and discernment are called for. Scrutinize your music.
Evaluate the intent and message. Most of all, ask God for a
discerning spirit. And if in doubt, stay on the safe side.

Positive mental attitude

The more humanistic and materialistic our society becomes, the
more appealing are the concepts of positive mental attitude, also
known as possibility thinking. People today don't generally seem
to be service oriented. Rather, they seem more interested in the
quest for success, looking inward in order to utilize their full
potential to advance themselves.

Of course, this doesn't mean that Christians should not be
success oriented. On the contrary. Jesus taught that we should
develop and utilize all our God-given talents (see Matthew 25:14-
30). The difference is twofold. First, Christians want to develop
their potential in order to serve others. Second, Christians rely on
a God outside of themselves, the true God, for their success—not on

an inherent power, or "power within." Like Paul, Christians say, "I can do all things *through Christ which strengtheneth me*" (Philippians 4:13). Moses warns those who feel they have become successful by their own efforts, "Remember the Lord thy God: for it is He that giveth thee power to get wealth" (Deuteronomy 8:18).

The fact is, there are two supernatural forces in this world: the divine force of God and the evil force of Satan. A person can achieve success under either. However, lasting and truly satisfying success can only be found in God's will for our lives. Satan's form of success is temporal, secular, and unsatisfying. The first is based on service and trust in God; the other on self, greed, and the love of money.

Western positive-mental-attitude gurus such as Horatio Alger, Samuel Clement Stone, Napoleon Hill, and Robert Schuller have promoted a philosophy that "whatever your mind can conceive, it can achieve." This is the basic premise upon which New Agers build their principles for success. And it works, for many have reached success using these principles. But it's also dangerous because it teaches that a person can pull himself up by his own bootstraps. The premise does not include Christ or the guidance of the Holy Spirit. It is based on the human mind, devoid of God, conceiving success and finding the means to achieve it. Some "Christian" seminars try to associate a positive mental attitude with biblical faith. This is a subtle lie that uses Christian terminology to disguise a secular or pagan belief. Such "faith" is no longer in God, but becomes the sheer force of the mind. Those who attempt to wed Christianity to the concepts of positive mental attitude teach that prayer can make things come to pass if only the person believes strongly enough. They make no mention of relying on God's will. Robert Schuller says:

> What is the magic ingredient that can ensure success and eliminate failure from our lives? It is FAITH! Possibility Thinking is just another word for faith. You don't know the power you have within you! . . . You can make the world into anything you choose. Yes, you can make the world into whatever you want it to be.[4]

From such false teachings, some conclude that prayer and faith are techniques for obtaining whatever they want. In place of the obligations or conditions that God has specified for answered prayer, they substitute the sheer force of the mind, the power within. Possibility thinking becomes an all-consuming, selfish venture that many find very lonely and disappointing in the end. The true premise is found in Scripture, "Trust in the Lord with all thine heart; and lean not unto thine own understanding. In all thy ways acknowledge Him, and He shall direct thy paths" (Proverbs 3:5, 6). "Ask, and it shall be given you; seek, and ye shall find; knock, and it shall be opened unto you" (Matthew 7:7). When these biblical principles are viewed and implemented in their original, God-intended manner, when we put Christ at the center of our lives, there is lasting, meaningful success.

The God who made us and who knows our potential also knows where we can achieve and excel the most. It is possible to achieve the heights He has set for our lives if we will trust Him, do His bidding, and follow His leading. Day by day He will reveal His plan for our lives as we seek Him in prayer.

Joseph, the son of Jacob in the Old Testament, is a good example. He learned two precious lessons early in his life that carried him to unimaginable success. First, he believed that there is an all-knowing God in heaven who is in control of the universe and everything that takes place in this world. That is the basic, profound truth that will start a person on the road to success. The second principle is like it: Joseph believed that God loved him and had a plan for his life. Therefore, he could trust God with his life. With these two divine principles, any person can achieve lasting and meaningful success in his Christian life. These are the foundational premises for true Christian "Positive Mental Attitude" and "Possibility Thinking."

The Christian road to success is based on Scripture and Christ; other prescriptions for success are not. In fact, Napoleon Hill claimed that a spirit entity gave him the secrets of success that he promised in his books.

The secrets of success that form the foundation for most success/motivation books and seminars were given to Hill by demons posing as "Masters who can disembody themselves and travel instantly to any place they choose." The "Supreme Secret" they authorized Hill to "reveal" to the world has been preserved in occult tradition for thousands of years and reminds one of the serpent's offer of godhood to

Eve: *Anything the human mind can believe, the human mind can achieve.* This seductive idea lies behind the Human Potential movement, which is another name for the New Age movement."[5]

I recall talking to a young graduate student who had been greatly influenced by the popular concepts depicted in "Positive Mental Attitude" books. He had subscribed to the principles for about two years and had achieved a measure of success for his age. But he came to the conclusion that it was void of God and was leading him away from Christ. In his view, those who learn and practice the principles of PMA believe they have no need of the Bible or Christ because they can do it on their own; that only weaklings or those who do not yet understand the principles of PMA need the Bible or Christ.

Horoscopes

Millions of people, including Christians, consult their horoscope readings daily, never dreaming where this seemingly innocent practice came from or where it can lead. The United States alone has an estimated 10,000 full-time and 175,000 part-time astrologers. More than two thousand newspapers carry daily horoscope readings.[6] A horoscope is a chart of the twelve signs of the zodiac by which an astrologer forecasts a person's destiny as determined by his birth date and the position of the planets and stars in conjunction with that date.

What should the Christian's attitude be regarding horoscope readings? Is it a harmless and innocent practice? Is it merely a game of foretelling the future?

No, it is no light matter.

Astrology, of which the horoscope is a part, is classified as an occult religion rather than a science. It is actually a form of planet worship. Astrology dates back to ancient Egypt. Aaron's golden calf in the wilderness (see Exodus 32:1-35) was nothing less than the Egyptian astrological god Taurus.

People read their horoscopes for one or all of the following reasons:

1. To learn what the future holds for them.
2. To be able to affect the future.
3. To anticipate and prepare for any given day.

4. To contact the spirits of the dead and universal entities.

5. To gain access to Satan and his demons.

Astrology essentially makes slaves of people; they get to the place that they can do nothing without consulting their horoscope. Even former president Ronald Reagan and his wife Nancy relied on astrological predictions. You may recall that it was Joan Quigley, the astrologer, who told Nancy when it was safe, according to the stars, for the president to travel.

Some of the modern-day religions that are heavily steeped in astrology are: the Rosicrucians, the Church of The Light, and the Theosophy Society. As Christians we are to look to Scripture and not to the stars. The stars and the planets declare God's handiwork (see Psalm 19:1), not our fate or future. Is it any wonder that astrology and the other occult practices were condemned by God (see Isaiah 47:13-15)?

Psychic counselors

You are probably aware of the sudden interest in psychic phenomena, if only through the number of TV commercials for psychics that are shown every day. One of the most popular TV psychic shows is Dionne Warwick's "Psychic Friends." Warwick takes people right from the audience and has her psychic friends do readings for them. The program also features testimonies by those who have been helped by her associates. After listening to the testimonies, the curiosity of the viewer runs high. The commercials then ask if the viewers have a difficult decision to make, or if they have financial, marital, career, or family problems. If so, they are urged to call the number on their TV screens to talk to a psychic in the privacy of their own living rooms. Everything will be kept confidential. These psychics are becoming wealthy, and also leading hundreds, perhaps thousands, of viewers into the occult world. Psychic readings and counseling come under the category of forbidden occult practices listed in Deuteronomy 18:10-12. They are part of New Age spiritualism and are among the fastest growing facets of the New Age movement.

Satanic New Age symbols

Symbols are powerful visual messages that can be used for good or for evil. Early Christians used the symbol of the fish to represent the church. Today the symbol of the dove, representing the Holy

Spirit, and the cross, representing salvation through Christ, are perhaps the most recognized symbols of Christianity. Similarly, the New Age movement has adopted many symbols to depict different aspects or philosophies of its system. Today's occult TV programs for children utilize many of these New Age symbols that children accept without realizing their satanic implications.

Surprisingly, one of the most widely used symbols of the New Age is the rainbow. New Agers have taken God's beautiful rainbow, stripped it of its biblical significance, and made it a symbol of bridging the gap between the conscious and the subconscious. The New Age rainbow also symbolizes man's evolutionary path, with its goal of exalting him to godhood, bridging the secular world and the New Age spirituality.

The peace symbol used by the hippies in the sixties is seen by some as nothing more than the inverted cross of Christ with its arms broken and encircled, symbolizing that it is held captive.

In children's TV cartoons, you'll see a lot of pentagrams—five-pointed stars. Wonder Woman, who performs magic and possesses supernatural powers, wears this symbol on the front of her headband. The pentagram is frequently identified with the occult. It is the symbol used for both black magic and white magic. When the encircled pentagram stands on one point, with two points pointing upward, and a goat's head superimposed on it, it is the symbol of Satan and black magic. When the encircled pentagram stands on two points, with one point on the top, and Adam superimposed on it, it represents white magic. Any time either of these two symbols are worn as jewelry or as patches on clothing, the wearer is, in effect, paying homage to Satan and his evil practices.

Triangles and pyramids

New Agers, especially those who are into the occult practices of witchery and satanism, venerate the triangle and the pyramid. It represents many things to them such as the unholy trinity: Osiris, father-god; Isis, mother-goddess; and Horus, their son-god.[7] Pyramids are believed to possess the qualities to perform magic.

J. Z. Knight, one of the most famous and well-known transchannelers, encountered her first vision of Ramtha, the spirit entity for whom she channels, while fooling around with construction-paper pyramids that she and her husband had made to capture some of these magical powers. She put one on her head, laughed, and pretended she was an Einstein genius. "I sure hope it works," she said.

Much to her surprise, the very next moment she saw a huge dazzling light at the other end of her kitchen. A hologram of a giant warrior appeared and said, "I am Ramtha, the Enlightened One. I have come to help you over the ditch [of human limitations and fears] . . . you will . . . beloved woman, become a light unto the world."[8] That was the beginning of her mystical relationship with the 3,500-year-old warrior who possesses her body and speaks through her, giving counsel to thousands—for a handsome fee, of course.

These symbols can be dangerous. They're nothing to play with or to take lightly. Even casually handling them with a curiosity about their magical, mystical potential could be the very first step that leads you into the occult world.

Crystals

Crystals are used widely by New Agers as a source of energy and power. Often they will incorporate crystals into necklaces; these become very personal and important to them because they believe these amethyst, quartz, or topaz crystals give them energy and balance. Crystals are used in holistic healing. Crystal healing is the practice of healing through the energy that crystals supposedly transmit to the body, aligning its electrical currents and thereby restoring a person to health. A sick person, or one who simply wishes to tone his electrical body currents, can accomplish this by laying a variety of crystals on his body for periods of time. Some New Agers even drink rock crystals ground into power, believing that this tonic can cure anything from a toothache to toenail fungus.

The crystal, especially the natural quartz formation, is the quintessential talisman of the New Age movement—as the cross is to Christianity.

Yin and Yang

One of the New Age symbols that has fascinated a wide variety of people is the Taoist "yin and yang" with New Age dots added. This symbol represents the unity and harmony of opposites. It is based on a philosophy totally contrary to Scripture. Yet many Christians, unaware of what they are promoting, wear this symbol as jewelry or display it in various ways. The Girl Scouts of America even have a proficiency badge ("The World in My Community") symbolized by the yin and yang.[9]

Symbols are very important, for they are tokens and emblems of philosophies and beliefs that the wearer or user espouses. It brings disgrace and discredit to God and His cause when Christians, knowingly or unknowingly, use or display these New Age symbols.

Rare is the person who has been able to escape the touch of the New Age through the various avenues identified in this book so far. The following chapter, however, will reveal a web in which many yet-untouched Christians may be caught. During an illness, a person's defenses may be down. Seeking health, he or she may become vulnerable to unscientific medical practices that can eventually lure them into a net of spiritual death.

1. *Time* magazine, 7 December 1987, 62.
2. Steven Halpern and Louis Savary, *Sound Health* (San Francisco: Harper & Row, 1985), 186.
3. Douglas Groothuis, *Confronting the New Age* (Downers Grove, Ill.: InterVarsity Press, 1988), 193.
4. Dave Hunt and T. A. McMahon, *The Seduction of Christianity* (Eugene, Ore.: Harvest House Publishers, 1985), 269.
5. Ibid., 19.
6. Robert A. Morey, *Horoscopes and the Christian* (Minneapolis, Minn.: Bethany House Publishers, 1981), 5.
7. Texe Marrs, *Mystery Mark of the New Age* (Westchester, Ill.: Crossway Books, 1988), 78.
8. J. Z. Knight, *A State of Mind*, 11, 12.
9. Texe Marrs, *Ravaged by the New Age* (Austin, Tex.: Living Truth Publishers, 1989), 66.

9

Holistic Medicine

A serious illness usually causes one to do in-depth thinking about spirituality, personal values, and the meaning of life and death. That is why health and illness can be key entryways into the New Age movement; New Agers are more than happy to supply their answers to these areas. Even in situations where health problems are not life threatening, New Agers take advantage of these opportunities by attempting to influence or indoctrinate patients with New Age views about wellness. And New Age holistic medicine is a most subtle and tricky area into which many unwary Christians can easily slip without even realizing it.

Suppose you have been visiting your conventional doctor for a year or more, but he hasn't been able to do anything with your back pains, stomach disorders, or the other ailments that make your life miserable. Then a friend glowingly recommends a doctor or a person who uses alternative health methods that have helped bring him relief from the same pains you are experiencing. You decide to check it out. During your visit, the person takes time to listen to you and shows interest in your total person, not just the symptoms. You feel that finally you have found someone who is concerned with you as a whole being and who is able to bring you some measure of relief. You aren't familiar with all the strange, mystical methods this person is employing or the concepts of reality he is explaining. Nevertheless, you decide to continue seeing him. Having done that, you have taken the first step into the New Age phenomena through the door of holistic medicine.

What is holistic medicine? It is one of the fastest-growing branches of the New Age movement. Many holistic medicine therapies focus on aligning the energies of the body under the belief that once the body is in line with cosmic energy, it will automatically heal itself. Some therapies, including hypnosis, imagery, and visualization, are based on the belief that by envisioning the body healing itself, the mind can bring about the actual cure without drugs or surgery. Other methods use crystal energy for healing, laying rock crystals of different kinds on prone bodies.

Why are millions of Americans turning to these New Age alternatives? Some are disenchanted with both the impersonal treatment and the high cost of mainstream medicine.[1] Others seek New Age alternatives because they are more "natural," and the mystical healing practices provide some relief from pain and sickness without the use of drugs. Still others seek out these pseudo-doctors and modern shamans because, having been diagnosed with a fatal disease for which conventional medicine offers no hope, they reach out in desperation to anyone or anything promising a cure.

Let's say you have a serious heart condition or cancer. Your doctor tells you that you have a 30-percent chance of recovery. Your treatments are painful and complex. Worst of all, you feel helpless because you can't do anything to improve your chances of recovery—except cooperate with the treatment. On the other hand, holistic health alternatives seem relatively painless and give you a measure of control over your situation.

Although some of these holistic "mind-cure" concepts may appear to be bizarre or even absurd, others are appealing to sincere Christians. Underlying beliefs of New Age medicine include monism (not to be confused with monotheism, which is a belief in one God) and pantheism. These two concepts are somewhat related.

Monism teaches that "all is one" and "one is all," that all reality, whether mind, matter, or any combination thereof, can be reduced to the same substance, essence, or principle. This reasoning leads to the belief that God and man are therefore the same or at least equal. "I am a god" is a New Age teaching.

Pantheism says that "all is God," that everything that exists is an all-inclusive unity and is divine. God is a force—a cosmic force or energy—that can assist in healing. He is an essence pervading everything in the universe. God is in the blade of grass, in the drop of rain, in the butterfly, in you and me. God is in everything living.

This concept destroys the belief in God as a personal Creator-God to whom we are subject. Instead, it puts man on the same plane with God.

"Holistic" is the New Age spelling for "wholistic," which refers to the whole body—physical, mental, and spiritual. While Christians also believe that human beings are a three-fold unity, and while Christians also believe in treating the whole person, they cannot adopt the underlying beliefs and philosophies of the New Age holistic medicine. On the surface some of these beliefs may seem to be similar to those held by Christians, but the underlying occult philosophies are still there, and are, in fact, even more dangerous because of their clever disguise. New Age health concepts involve:

1. belief in an impersonal force as opposed to the omnipotence of a personal God;
2. attempting to allow the body to heal itself through manipulating energy, thereby denying the power of God, the ultimate Healer;
3. using the human mind to create reality, thus preempting the prerogative of the Creator.

New Age holistic medicine covers a spectrum of alternative healing; some writers list as many as fifty such treatments. Some of the more common ones are: acupuncture, acupressure, biofeedback, crystal healing, homeopathy, hypnosis, iridology, naturopathy, reflexology, psychic surgery, therapeutic touch, guided imagery, macrobiotics, and yoga. These can be categorized in five areas: (1) self-healing (what is perceived is more important than the disease), (2) prevention (through diet, herbs, mixing of foods), (3) imagery (the power of suggestion, visualization), (4) nutrition (growing, preparation, and storing food), and (5) bodywork (balancing mind and body to retain health).[2]

Let's take a look at some of these treatments and their claims.

Biofeedback

This is the technique of bringing normally involuntary bodily functions or processes under conscious mental control. Through the use of special electronic monitoring devices and mental exercises, biofeedback attempts to train a person to consciously control such involuntary bodily functions as blood flow, breathing, and heartbeat. For example, in treating migraine headaches, the artery that contracts and restricts blood flow to the brain and then spontaneously dilates, causing pain, is brought under conscious control through the powers of the mind and imaging. The patient is taught to actually change the temperature of the fingers through consciously controlling the flow of blood to these areas, thereby averting the headache. Although this self-therapy method may indeed produce results, it can also lead a person into occult metaphysical beliefs and practices. Some doctors using biofeedback make inappropriate claims and employ various forms of mind-altering practices. A friend went to three doctors using biofeedback techniques; two of them tried to get him into visualizing during meditation. He was totally repulsed by what they asked him to do and refused to engage in the visualization exercises. He sensed that something was not right and resisted.

"Dr. Green of the Menninger Foundation developed the procedure of biofeedback by investigating trance states of Hindu yogis, observing how they mentally controlled internal body functions during altered states of consciousness."[3] Dr. Green and his wife Alice are pioneer biofeedback researchers and admit that biofeedback creates the same state of consciousness and results as yoga. In fact, biofeedback has been called the high-tech "yoga of the West." And yoga is considered dangerous for those who are not properly trained or experienced with the techniques when they practice this ancient Hindu art.

It may be that the purest forms of biofeedback have a valid place in the treatment of such conditions as migraine headaches and high blood pressure. However, extreme caution should be taken in selecting a therapist and participation in questionable exercises should be avoided.

Acupuncture and acupressure

These ancient Chinese Taoist medical practices are based on the philosophy of the mystical unity of the yin and yang—the psychic or cosmic life energy forces in the body. According to the Chinese, good and ill health depend on the proportional strengths or harmonious flow of these forces.

Taoists believe that the body is a microcosm of the yin and yang. The yang is the white, or light side, of the yin/yang symbol and represents the macrocosm of the universe—sun and light, the warm and dry, the positive and good, masculinity, procreation, and strength. It is the south side of a hill, as the Chinese would say.

The north side of a hill, or dark side, is the yin. It represents the microcosm or the earth, the shadow or darkness, the negative, evil principle in nature, the female, and wickedness. Taoism teaches that harmony comes about through the proper balance of these two opposites, the harmony of the positive and negative, light and darkness, evil and good. When sickness occurs, it is believed that there is a disruption of this energy life-force flow. To restore health, these psychic life forces must be unclogged and allowed to flow freely again. The needles or the fingertips of an acupressurist are supposed to cause this to happen, thereby restoring the balance of the two cosmic energies in the body.

Some say that there are 365 acupuncture points on the body. Others say there are as many as a thousand. These points are located on what are called the twelve meridians or channels in the body, corresponding to the twelve months of the year or the twelve areas of the universe.

Acupuncture and acupressure are very similar. The one employs hair-pin needles, and the other, the pressure of fingers on the areas where stimulation is desired. Some of the needles are extremely fine, about one one-hundredth of an inch in diameter and can be as long as four inches. The roots of acupuncture and acupressure however, are found in Taoist philosophy and religion.

Karen Hoyt is executive director of Spiritual Counterfeits Projects, a Christian, nonprofit corporation established to research and provide information on new religious movements. She says:

> Some Christian practitioners who use these New Age techniques argue that they are simply making use of a neutral phenomenon (as electricity is neutral). They say the fact that we don't understand why something works shouldn't automatically consign a practice to a realm of the occult. Some even claim to have "recaptured" the techniques from the New Age camp, and thus put them to work for godly purposes. This is, unfortunately, easier said than proven, especially when the concept is a basic precept of a religious system.[4]

Another Christian writer states:

Satanic agents claim to cure disease. They attribute their power to electricity, magnetism, or the so-called "sympathetic remedies," while in truth they are but channels for Satan's electric currents. By this means he casts his spell over the bodies and souls of men.[5]

In Portland, Oregon, 256 arrested drug users participated in a fourteen-day acupuncture treatment program to help them cope with the effects of withdrawal. "Acupuncture does work," said James Hennings, head of Metropolitan Public Defender, Inc., an office representing most of the defendants. "It's like black magic. I can't tell you why it works, but it seems to."[6] To associate the results of acupuncture with black magic may be too reckless and irresponsible for some. Even though acupuncture is not scientific or physiologically logical, the thing that makes it dangerous is that it comes from an occult, pagan philosophy.

The yin and yang philosophy of the unity or harmony of the two opposites permeates all of Taoist thinking; it is pagan and diametrically opposed to the Scriptures. The Bible teaches that in order to restore lasting peace and harmony, the Christian must separate himself from evil, not seek a proper balance between them, as Taoists teach. God tells us to separate ourselves from evil, to be pure, consecrated, and holy. The mingling of good and evil is what has brought about the sinful, degraded condition which exists on the earth.

Reflexology

Reflexology is based on the belief that the feet contain the nerve endings which lead to the different organ and body parts. Manipulation of various points on the feet are thought to clear pathways for the energy to flow, thereby bringing health to the affected part. "At best, reflexology gives a good massage. At worst, it can be a form of psychic development and energy channeling. Medically, it is useless."[7] Reflexology's roots are in the occult, and its techniques are based on the principle of a life force being present within the body that can be manipulated by massage to enhance health.

Iridology

Iridology is used as a diagnostic tool and operates on the principle that the iris of the eye reveals the health condition, both past and present, of each part of the body. Both reflexology and iridology began with pagan, shamanistic healing methods.[8]

In 1979 the *Journal of the American Medical Association* published the results of a study conducted by three ophthalmologists. One hundred and forty-three patients' eyes were studied to determine if the iris was a reliable diagnostic tool. Forty-three patients were known to have kidney disease; ninety-five were free from the disease.

The results revealed that there is "no value in iridology as a screening technique for detecting or diagnosing kidney disease."[9] Further, the findings reported that patients who rely on an iridologist as a diagnosis for kidney disease could be harmed by unnecessary delay in detection and lack of proper treatment.

Homeopathy

This treatment method relies on spiritual and energy forces for healing. The concept: Everything in the universe is one and the same—all is one. Attempts to stimulate the body's healing ability are made by treating the disease with small doses of otherwise harmful medicine.

Another avenue through which Christians are being attracted to holistic medicine is through diet and nutrition. Many Christians are very health conscious, and by endeavoring to improve their quality of life and longevity, they become easy prey for the "natural" approaches of New Age health. The New Age approach teaches prevention of disease by proper diet, food production, preparation, and storage, but this is only an opening door for the introduction of its underlying spiritual philosophies.

Michael Harner, in his book *A Guide to Power and Healing* , says,

> The burgeoning field of holistic medicine shows a tremendous amount of experimentation involving the reinvention of many techniques long practiced in shamans such as visualization, altered state of consciousness, aspects of psychoanalysis, hypnotherapy, meditation, positive attitudes, stress reduction, and mental and emotional expression of personal will for help and healing. In a sense, shamanism is being reinvented in the West precisely because it's needed.[10]

Macrobiotics

Macrobiotics is defined as the "study of prolonging life, as by special diets, etc."[11] This attempt to bring about health through diet also operates on the Taoist view of universal energy and harmony between opposites. It places great emphasis on balancing the food intake to combat disease. It has been billed as a cancer cure, but without proven evidence.

But macrobiotics is more than a diet. It is a way of life. Eating macrobiotically, it is claimed, puts a person in harmony with universal energy. Along with the diet, one must also have daily exercise and practice Eastern meditation and prayer.

Naturopathy

Those advocating naturopathy hold that people are poisoning themselves with what they eat. They teach purification through diet, purging, internal cleansing, and mind control.

Naturopathy employs a wide range of New Age treatments having occultic potential such as radionics, homeopathy, meditation, and yoga. Thus, naturopathy may inhibit correct diagnosis of a problem, permitting a curable illness to assume serious or incurable proportions; it may also offer ineffective treatments and involve clients in occultic methods."[12]

Another holistic health approach to those seeking good health is through mind therapy. Whether taught as stress relievers, mind relaxers, or ways of accelerating recovery, the underlying principles are dangerous.

Yoga

Offered as an exercise discipline, yoga is a Hindu philosophical and religious system whose practices lead toward the goal of union with Brahma, a Hindu god.

Although the public falsely perceives yoga as a safe or neutral practice, even authoritative yoga literature is replete with warnings of serious physical consequences, mental derangement, and harmful spiritual effects. Paralysis, insanity, and death are frequently mentioned. Allegedly, such consequences arise from *wrong* yoga practice, but, in fact, they really arise because yoga is an *occult* practice. Those who care about their overall health should not practice yoga."[13]

If you have been innocently led into any of these nontraditional New Age medical practices, it would be advisable for you to ask God to give you a discerning spirit. Ask questions and scrutinize closely any unfamiliar concepts. Then, ask God for courage to break with those practices that are connected in any way with mystical or occult philosophies.

In a 1988 study done by the National Opinion Research Council of the University of Chicago it was discovered that 67 percent of those questioned believed in the supernatural; 42 percent claimed they had been in contact with the dead; and 23 percent expressed belief in the concept of reincarnation.[14] All of these beliefs are present in alternative New Age medical practices. And Christians are emphatically forbidden to have anything to do with them (see Deuteronomy 18:10-12)!

Potential dangers

Apart from the biblical injunction to avoid these practices, there are several other potential dangers or risks of involvement with alternative medicine.

1. Physical harm. A late diagnosis or lack of treatment may lead to great physical harm. Some reason, "Alternative medical therapy may help, and even if it doesn't, at least it won't hurt to try." But such thinking may lead to postponing a legitimate medical diagnosis until it is too late. On the other hand, when disease has run its course and done its damage, holistic medicine is still not a substitute for surgery or needed medication.

Holistic medicine claims to be natural, more down to earth and spiritual. The word *natural* implies that it is healthful or safe. However, *natural* as used by the New Agers is misleading, as the term may include methods connected with the occult. Many of the so-called natural holistic health therapies do not agree with the natural laws of God. In some cases establishing correct habits in one's lifestyle is enough to restore declining health.

Nutritional deficiencies can occur from stringent diets such as the macrobiotic diet. Also, some of these therapies rely on untested, questionable ingredients that can cause physical harm, as can the toxic effects of contaminated substances such as bacteria and fungi in herbs not governed by the U.S. Food and Drug Administration.

2. Emotional harm. Not all who see New Age doctors and medical practitioners find healing. In fact, only about half do, most of whom are prone to be receptive to these pseudo-health treatments. Dr. Norman Shealy states that acupuncture is effective for pain only about 30 percent of the time.[15]

In some alternative methods, responsibility for the disease is placed on the patient. Because "reality is only what you perceive it to be," the patient is told that he caused the disease in the first place. Therefore, he must be responsible for curing it. Accepting this responsibility can lead to guilt and self-incrimination if healing does not occur.

Alternative practitioners teach a concept of "mind over disease." Reality is relative; it's whatever you perceive it to be.[16] So think yourself well. Actual denial of disease is a Christian Scientist belief.[17]

Hypnosis in therapy can lead to the weakening of the powers of the mind and eventual control of your mind by someone else.

3. Spiritual harm. One of the most dangerous aspects of alternative medicine is its mystical religious roots and occult philosophies. In order to see the dangers of this New Age tentacle of deception one must look beneath the surface to its gnarled roots deeply imbedded in occult and pagan religious beliefs. The philosophies on which these practices are based come from the occult, Hinduism, and Taoism (such as the yin and yang philosophy, aligning of the life energies, stimulating the chakras, and introspective Eastern meditation).

And practitioners of alternative medicine are not inhibited in telling their patients about these concepts. People who are ill are often desperate and therefore more vulnerable to spiritual indoctrination. Involvement entices one to become further involved with mystical, occult practices—often without realizing it. If you are indeed "healed" by an alternative health method, chances are that you will be more open to investigate the philosophies behind the therapies and in time become a believer.

Those who give themselves up to the sorcery of Satan, may boast of great benefit received, but does this prove their course to be wise or safe? What if life should be prolonged? What if temporal gain should be secured? Will it pay in the end to have disregarded the will of God? All such apparent gain will prove at last an irrevocable loss.[18]

Some Christians rationalize that they can deal with error in the philosophies of alternative medicine by just spitting out the bad.[19] But it is not as easy to separate the good from the bad as one might think.

Some Christians feel they can use such therapies without buying into the philosophies behind them, claiming that a neutral phenomenon of God's creation has been misinterpreted by ancient mystics and New Agers. In light of the scarcity of evidence that these "life energies" actually exist, such a belief represents wishful thinking. Questions or criticism are often deflected by a lame rationale: "I don't understand it; I just know it works." Unfortunately, those who feel they have been helped by an energy therapy are likely to be open to the New Age movement's explanations.[20]

The Bible says, "Does a fountain send forth at the same place sweet water and bitter?" (James 3:11). Job 14:4 says, "Who can bring a clean thing out of an unclean? Not one."

Examples of alternative forms of treatment that must be rejected include homeopathy, reflexology, iridology, pendulum therapy, and treatments associated with spurious philosophies of astrology, yoga, yin-yang, and spiritism. These are not only unproven but are totally irrational from an understanding of human anatomy and physiology. Those associated with psychic phenomena have serious spiritual implications.[21]

Reincarnation seeks to replace the Christian belief in eternal life. The Western version of reincarnation is an upward spiral toward perfection that also teaches the satanic lie, "You shall not die." New Age medicine "proves" this theory with near-death-experiences (NDE). But these NDEs are very similar to shamanistic journeys and contact with spirits.

At a recent camp meeting, I spoke on the dangers of holistic medicine. At the conclusion of my presentation, several people lined up to speak with me. About half thanked me for alerting them to the dangers that holistic health poses to one's spiritual well-being. The other half expressed deep concern about one or two areas I had dealt with. They, or a relative or friend, were involved in acupressure, reflexology, or iridology. Some had received certain New Age medical treatments, or in a few cases were even themselves administering some of these treatments to others. Some said they could see nothing wrong with the practices, claiming that most of the time they had brought healing and relief from their pain.

One gentleman said, "It doesn't matter to me where these practices come from. They work, and that's all I'm concerned with." But healing is not always proof that alternative New Age medicine is credible or safe to use. Karen Hoyt cautions:

> We have been clearly warned not to deal with the supernatural, except in direct communication with God through prayer. Any other interactions are not only forbidden, but also frankly hazardous. We do not have to read far in scripture to learn that the spiritual realm is not all sweetness and light. One-third of its inhabitants are described as powerful, cunning and destructive. Tampering directly with their turf is as about intelligent as learning to swim in a lagoon full of great white sharks.[22]

Satan can employ his powers to bring sickness, accident, and death. Or he can bring relief. Bob Larson, in his book *Straight Answers on the New Age*, explains how:

> Satan is prepared to promise physical health in exchange for disobedience to God. . . . He temporarily relieves physical affliction by transferring the malady to the emotional, psychic realm. Those who have been to New Age healers often experience assuagement of physical pain, but usually it is followed by emotional torment or an accentuated interest in the occult, drawing them deeper into the devil's snare. Thus, New Age healing, which denies Christ as Creator, Redeemer, and Healer, merely exchanges an adversity on the

organic level for torment on the spiritual level.[23]

So, while it is true that there may be some temporary external benefits from using these practices, they do not come without a price. And the price one pays may be more than monetary. It could mean the selling of your soul in exchange for physical health and healing.

1. John Ankerberg and John Weldon, *The Facts on Holistic Health and the New Medicine* (Eugene, Oreg.: Harvest House Publishers, 1992), 5.
2. Bob Larson, *Straight Answers on the New Age* (Nashville, Tenn.: Thomas Nelson Publishers, 1989), 82.
3. Larson, *Straight Answers on the New Age*, 249.
4. Karen Hoyt, *The New Age Rage* (Old Tappan, N.J.: Fleming H. Revell Company, 1977), 69.
5. Ellen G. White, *Evangelism* (Washington,D.C.: Review and Herald Publishing Association, 1946), 609.
6. The *Oregonian*, 25 March 1992.
7. Ankerberg and Weldon, 41.
8. Larson, *Straight Answers on the New Age*, 93, 94.
9. *JAMA: Journal of the American Medical Association*, 242 (18 September 1979), 1389.
10. Michael Harner, *A Guide to Power and Healing: The Way of the Shaman* (New York: Barton Publishers, 1980), xiii, as quoted in David Sneed and Sharon Sneed, *The Hidden Agenda: A Critical View of Alternative Medical Therapies* (Nashville, Tenn.: Thomas Nelson Publishers, 1982), 195.
11. *Webster's New World Dictionary*, s.v. "macrobiotics."
12. Ankerberg and Weldon, 37.
13. Ibid.
14. Sneed and Sneed, *Hidden Agenda*, 224.
15. C. Norman Shealy, *Occult Medicine Can Save Your Life* (Alpharetta, Ga.: Ariel Press, 1975), 163.
16. Sneed and Sneed, *Hidden Agenda*, 47.
17. Ibid.
18. Ellen G. White, *Evangelism*, 606, 607.
19. Sneed and Sneed, *Hidden Agenda*, 41.
20. Karen Hoyt, *The New Age Rage* (Old Tappan, N.J.: Fleming H. Revell Company, 1978), 65.
21. Albert Whiting, "Alternative Forms of Treatment," pamphlet from Health and Temperance Department of the General Conference of Seventh-day Adventists (August 1991), 2.
22. Karen Hoyt, *The New Age Rage*, 64.
23. Bob Larson, *Straight Answers on the New Age*, 78.

CHAPTER

10

The Emerging New World Order

It was a meeting destined to change the course of history! Two world leaders from vastly different geographical, cultural, and religious backgrounds, but with one common interest, met face to face for the first time. It was a secret meeting, lasting only fifty minutes, but its effects would be felt for years to come and would directly or indirectly affect the governments of many countries on both sides of the world. The meeting's purpose: to conceive a strategy that would ultimately affect the lives of millions living under Communist rule in Eastern Europe. This historical meeting was the inception of what later became known as the Holy Alliance between the Vatican and the United States.

This clandestine conference took place on Monday, June 7, 1982, in the Vatican library between then–U.S. president Ronald Reagan and Pope John Paul II. Just the year before, both had survived an assassin's bullet within six weeks of each other, and it was their firm belief that God had spared their lives for a special mission. *Time* magazine quoted Reagan as saying to a close friend, "Look how the evil forces were put in our way and how Providence intervened."[1] President Reagan and Pope John Paul II discussed several international concerns, but at the heart of their conversation was the pope's concern over Communist rule in his native Poland and in the rest of Eastern Europe.

Going on at the same time, in an adjacent room, was a meeting of Agostino Cardinal Casaroli and Archbishop Achille Silvestrini with Secretary of State Alexander Haig and Judge William Clark,

Reagan's national security advisor. Interestingly, these Reagan men, as well as other key players (William Casey, Allen Walters, and William Wilson, the first ambassador to the Vatican), were all devout Roman Catholics and regarded this relationship as a holy alliance.[2]

The master plan of this alliance, which did not become public knowledge until almost ten years later when *Time* magazine published it on February 24, 1992, was to overthrow Communist rule in Poland by secretly supporting the Solidarity Movement. If this could be accomplished, these men reasoned, the rest of Eastern Europe would follow.

Consequently, millions of dollars and tons of computers, word processors, and fax machines "were smuggled into Poland via channels established by priests, American agents, representatives of the AFL-CIO, and European labor movements. Money for the banned union came from CIA funds, the National Endowment for Democracy, secret accounts in the Vatican, and western trade unions."[3]

By 1988, Mikhail Gorbachev, then president of the now-defunct Soviet Union, made a trip to Poland and acknowledged that Warsaw could not rule Poland without Solidarity's cooperation. On April 5, 1989, Solidarity was legalized. Nine years after Lech Walesa had been arrested and Solidarity banned, Communist rule was overthrown and Tadeusz Mazowiecki became prime minister of Poland. It was only a matter of time after Solidarity's triumph over Communism that a domino effect rapidly spread throughout Eastern Europe. On November 16, 1989, the infamous Berlin Wall was toppled, along with East Germany's Communist government. Shortly thereafter, and most surprisingly of all, the seventy-four-year reign of Communism in Russia came to an end in 1991 with the disintegration of the Soviet Union and the election of Boris Yeltsin, the first freely-elected leader in Russia in over a thousand years.[4]

This Holy Alliance, many feel, was the catalyst that precipitated the downfall of Communism. However, some credit the pope with having masterminded the whole affair with an eye toward a "New World Order."[5] After the Tiananmen Square demonstration in June 1989, the Beijing government, fearful that what happened to Eastern Europe and the Soviet Union could also happen to China, proclaimed the pope as China's Public Enemy Number One. There are an estimated seven million Catholics in China, many of whom are meeting clandestinely with papal leaders. But it's China's young people who have the government scared. These young people saw what the Catholic Church was able to do in Eastern Europe and Russia, and they are now joining the church. "Just like in Eastern Europe, religion becomes a way of fighting back without fighting."[6] China has good reason to fear the New World Order for John Paul II's philosophy calls for more than spiritual unity. This blueprint includes "a new society of peoples and nations undivided by nationalism, cultural diversity, wealth or poverty, political systems or religious hatred."[7]

Former Jesuit priest Malachi Martin, in his book *The Keys of This Blood—A Struggle for World Dominion between Pope John Paul II, Mikhail Gorbachev and the Capitalist West*, describes this new world order as the "first one-world system of government that has ever existed in the society of nations."[8] Martin continues by stating that whoever leads the New World Order "will hold the authority and wield the dual power of authority and control over each of us as individuals and over all of us as a community; over the entire six billion people expected by the demographers to inhabit the earth by early in the third millennium."[9]

Such statements ought to concern us because this scenario is not something in the far-distant future. According to Martin, it is imminent and predicted to take place in the final decade of the second millennium. "Those of us who are under seventy will see at least the basic structures of the new world government installed. Those of us under forty will surely live under its legislative, executive and judiciary authority and control."[10]

Contenders for leadership

But who will give leadership to the New World Order? According to Martin, there *were* three contenders: Mikhail Gorbachev, the Western capitalist world under the leadership of the U.S. president, and Pope John Paul II. But, Martin says, the pope is the only person qualified and destined to lead the New World Order because:

1. as claimant to the title "Vicar of Christ," the Polish pope is the "ultimate court of judgment on the society of states as a society"[11];

2. John Paul II is the sole possessor of the ecclesiastical world authority invested in him through the keys "washed in the human blood of the God-Man, Jesus Christ"[12];

3. the Vatican leader is the only contender whose moral principles are rooted in the teachings of Christ which "is the backbone principle of the New World Order envisaged by the Pontiff."[13]

At this juncture I should point out that Martin's 517-page book has no footnotes and no bibliography. It is listed neither as fiction or nonfiction. Instead, it comes under a new category called "faction." It is a book expressing the mind of the pope and the author, written in an attempt to impose their views on the readers. Be careful how you use his book.

Mikhail Gorbachev has also espoused New Age philosophies for a New World Order. His book, *Perestroika* ("restructuring"), published in 1989, was on the best-seller list for two years. In it, he calls for political and structural change, not only for Russia but for the world. In fact, the subtitle to his book is, "New Thinking for Our Country and the World."

Looking back, there is no doubt that Gorbachev was instrumental in laying the groundwork for the dismantling of Communism in his world domain. He was a modern Cyrus, perhaps, whose glory was short-lived. Now, with Gorbachev's exit in 1991 from the scene of international politics, the contest for world leadership has narrowed to two. But here we find no competition because these two powers—the Vatican and the United States—have formed a Holy Alliance, which is still alive and well. In fact, "Windows on Washington" reported that when George Bush was president, he and Pope John Paul II discussed world affairs on the telephone "at least once a week."[14]

The United States in prophecy

Many view the forming of this Holy Alliance as a fulfillment of the Bible prophecy in Revelation 13:11-17. In this passage, John describes a lamblike beast power emerging out of the earth and declares that it will eventually enforce the authority of "the first beast"—Rome (see verses 11, 12).

Since the mid-1800s, some Bible students have identified this lamblike "beast coming up out of the earth" (verse 11) with the United States of America. Seventh-day Adventist leader J. N. Andrews made this identification in an 1851 issue of *The Advent Review and Sabbath Herald*. Ellen White confirmed that the second beast of Revelation 13 was indeed Protestant America in the 1884 edition of *The Great Controversy*. Andrews came to his conclusion because the United States fulfills the following requirements of this prophecy:

1. The timing. The United States was beginning to grow into prominence at the time the first beast power described in Revelation 13:1-10 received its "deadly wound," when French general Berthier took Pope Pius VI into captivity in 1798.

2. The location. The United States arose in a scarcely populated area of the world, represented by the "earth" in the prophecy, whereas the "first beast" (Rome) arose from the sea, which, according to Revelation 17:15, represents peoples and nations—a heavily populated area such as central Europe.

3. Its characteristics. The two horns of the lamblike beast depict religious and civil liberty, the basic fundamental freedoms guaranteed by the U.S. Constitution and establishing the separation of church and state.

4. Its actions. This lamblike power, according to the prophecy, would speak "as a dragon" (Revelation 13:11) and give power and authority to the first beast, Rome (see verses 12-15).

Andrews and others in the nineteenth century accepted this last point by faith. The United States was not yet the world superpower it would become. Only faintly could they discern this nation speaking "as a dragon" and reestablishing the power of the Roman papacy. Today we can perhaps see the outlines more plainly. America has become the acknowledged leader of world power, and even more significantly, an American president and a Roman pontiff have entered into a Holy Alliance.

Since the end of World War II, America has been contending with the Soviet Union for first place as the world's superpower. Today the cold war is over—won by the West under the leadership of the United States. After the 1991 Gulf War, in which America led a coalition of thirteen countries against Iraq, the United States emerged as *the* world superpower, militarily and politically.[15]

It was during this crisis and after that George Bush began talking about a "new world order," attempting to solidify this globalist concept in the minds of people both here and around the world. Since then new words and phrases have come into vogue such as "global consciousness"; "global community"; "geopolitical structure"; "mega-religionists," etc.

The coalition of countries that fought against Iraq in the Gulf War was an example of what a new world order of nations could do when the well-being and peace of another country (or of the world) is threatened. George Bush says, "The New World Order describes a responsibility imposed by our successes . . . working with other nations to: deter aggression, achieve stability, achieve prosperity, achieve peace."[16] Of course, if the people in government read the same Bible you and I read, they would know that none of these things are going to happen in a lasting way in our world until Jesus establishes the new earth at the end of the millennium.

> The day of the Lord will come as a thief in the night; in the which the heavens shall pass away with a great noise, and the elements shall melt with fervent heat, the earth also and the works that are therein shall be burned up. . . . Nevertheless we, according to his promise, look for new heavens and a new earth, wherein dwelleth righteousness (2 Peter 3:10, 13).

In this world, no human leader, or leaders, will ever establish lasting world peace. Read it for yourself in 1 Thessalonians 5:3: "For when they shall say, peace and safety; then sudden destruction cometh upon them." This is not a pessimistic way of looking at our end-time existence on earth. It is God reminding us that this world is not our permanent home. We are just passing through. This present corrupt world will end. All things will be made new. The meek will inherit the earth, and the pure in heart shall see God (see Revelation 21:4; Matthew 5:5, 8).

After the war with Iraq, Yassir Arafat, the Palestinian leader, referred to Washington, D.C. as "the New Rome."[17] Whether he realized it or not, his reference was significant. Why "the *New* Rome"? Because the old Rome was the unrivaled super-religious and political power of its time. Now America is the super-political power—and according to the prophecy it will enforce the religious dictates of Rome.

It may surprise you to know that New Agers believe the Age of Aquarius—the age we are supposedly entering at present—requires a New World Order.

The religious right in America
Another element in this New World Order scenario is the Christian Coalition, composed mainly of evangelical believers, even though it includes Catholics and Jews. This coalition is more

influential and determined than Jerry Falwell's Moral Majority ever was. The Christian Coalition's second annual "Road to Victory Conference and Strategy Briefing" was held on September 11 and 12, 1992, at Founders' Inn Conference Center in Virginia Beach, Virginia. The five hundred delegates included Dan Quayle, Oliver North, William Bennett, U.S. secretary of education Lamar Alexander, and many more Washington bright stars.

The Christian Coalition's ultimate goal is to restore America to greatness under God through moral strength.[18] At the gala banquet, Pat Robertson declared, "The recent major natural disasters: the San Francisco earthquake, Hurricane Andrew and Hurricane Iniki, are evidences that God is displeased with the wickedness of our nation. We can expect these disasters to increase until we get our nation back to God."[19] Although this may sound pious and good, a strong suspicion persists among many that the Christian Coalition's tolerance for differing religious views and beliefs will be nil.

Attorney Keith Fournier, executive director of the American Center for Law and Justice, began his address to this group by saying, "I am a Catholic; this may surprise some of you, but we are all in this together."[20] He went on to boldly challenge the First Amendment by stating: "The wall of separation between Church and State that was erected by secular humanists and other enemies of religious freedom, has to come down. That wall is more of a threat to society than the Berlin wall ever was."[21]

A New World Order

The ultimate goal of the New Age movement is to bring about utopia, a global community of peace, love, and prosperity. Marilyn Ferguson, author of *The Aquarian Conspiracy*, quotes from Victor Hugo's prophecy about the twentieth century, when "wars would die, frontier boundaries would die, dogma would die . . . and man would live."[22] This is the age we are supposedly entering with the Age of Aquarius. But in order for all this to come to fruition, a paradigm shift must take place—an entirely new way of looking at our world. Ferguson says we need to see the whole earth as a "jewel in space, a fragile water planet . . . without natural borders. It is not the globe of high school days with its many-colored nations." She continues, "The old ways are untenable. All countries are economically and ecologically involved with each other, politically enmeshed. The old gods of isolationism and nationalism are tumbling artifacts like the stone deities of Easter Island."[23]

New Age teachers are teaching citizenship education far differently than they were when many of us went to school. Today citizenship education is taught with a global emphasis, pointing out "the shortcomings of our nation and the wonderful vision of the future world-society," stressing that "nation-states have outlived their usefulness and a New World Order is necessary if we are to live in harmony with each other."[24]

Thus New Age teachers see themselves as key crusaders for the New World Order to take place in the Age of Aquarius. They see themselves as citizens of a global community. The concept of the New World Order is that of a globalistic, socialistic society, not a free, democratic one. It is a society in which the rights of minorities must be sacrificed for the good of the whole community.

John Lennon of the Beatles—and one of the greatest rock idols of all time—promoted this dream of a one-world society in his well-known song, *Imagine*. The lyrics say, "Imagine all the people sharing all the world." Lennon sang of a world without a heaven or a hell, a world leaving God completely out of the picture. Another line in the song says, "You may say I'm a dreamer, but I'm not the only one." And Lennon was correct. Many in the sixties were closet New Age believers, and this song brought them into the open. It stimulated the thinking of the masses of his young admirers, many of whom are at the forefront of the New Age movement today.

But is this New World Order really all that its proponents claim it will be? When the "old Rome" was in power, there was fierce persecution for those who would not comply with its dictates. Yassir Arafat may not have known all that his description implied prophetically when he referred to Washington, D.C. as "the New Rome." But the New World Order, of which the Holy Alliance is a part, will demand the same compliance and conformity from the citizens of the world as did Rome in ages past. In order for the world to survive politically, economically, ecologically, and socially, it is proposed that a single global government is imperative. The people of this world will have to give up their national barriers and allegiances as well as their unique religious beliefs. Revelation 13:15-17 predicts that this lamblike beast (the United States) will require the entire world to give allegiance to the first beast (Rome) and that those who will not comply by receiving the "mark" of the beast, will not be able to buy or sell. Those who will not worship the image of the beast will be killed. The religious freedoms now guaranteed by the U.S. Constitution, will obviously be reversed.

The ecological movement

Another event in this mosaic of the New World Order is the Earth Summit held June 3-14, 1992 in Rio de Janeiro, Brazil with 178 countries participating. Although the main agenda was ecological responsibility and eradication of poverty, the distinguished gathering of government heads posed a natural setting to discuss world unification. In fact, one of the concepts that emerged from this meeting was that in order to save the planet, we must work in unity as one global community—a sort of global Marshall Plan. And the way to accomplish this unity is a new world government with legal power over all nations. This idea is being seriously considered by politically powerful people today more than ever before. Vice-president Al Gore says, "A global Marshall Plan, if you will, is now urgently needed."[25]

Christians haven't been alarmed by the growing popularity of the ecological movement. In fact, many consider it a worthy cause, and of course its basic premise of concern for the earth is in harmony with Christian concepts of mankind's stewardship over the earth. However, many ecologists give a religious personification to nature; nature is seen as Mother Earth, "Gaia"—the pagan goddess of the earth, the spirit that inhabits plants, etc. The New Age encourages men and women to return to their sense of being a part of nature. They do not encourage human beings to return to God, the Creator of nature, but to nature itself. Vice-president Al Gore, a passionate defender of the environment for more than twenty years, argues that only a radical rethinking of our relationship with nature can save the earth's ecology for future generations. Environmentalists, such as Gore, believe we are destroying our world because we are out of touch with Mother Earth. The real problem is that we are out of touch with God who created our earth.

While environmental protection is a legitimate concern, this growing movement could become a common rallying point, together with the concern for global peace, on which diverse governments and religions could agree in the effort for global unity. This possibility was demonstrated at the 1992 Earth Summit. In fact, "The World Council of Churches has now decided that the major test of orthodoxy is one's position on the environment."[26]

One of the most influential religious groups at the Summit was the Baha'i International Community, which prepared a document entitled "Elements for Inclusion in the Proposed Earth Charter." Their recommendation:

> Nothing short of a world federal system, guided by universally agreed upon and enforceable laws, will allow nation states to manage cooperatively an increasingly interdependent and rapidly changing world, thereby ensuring peace and social and economic justice for all the world's peoples.[27]

The pieces coming together

So, where does the New Age movement fit into all this? According to Tal Brooke, in his book *When the World Will Be As One*,

> the New Age movement is the spiritual structure for globalism; it is a critically important adhesive to hold all of the other elements in place. As a spiritual system, naturally it must have its human agents—its mouth pieces in contact with powers beyond this world. . . . Clearly a plan is unfolding. It has everything in the world to do with the New World Order.[28]

The New Age movement has as its basic premise the monistic philosophy "All is one." There are no distinctions of opposites, consciousness applies to all nature, and all reality is only energy. This philosophy extends further to apply to nations. All national boundaries should disappear in order to form a one-world government with a one-world religion. This New Age religion, no doubt, would resemble Eastern religious beliefs rather than Western, since that element is already predominant in the New Age. The Maastricht Treaty envisioning a unified European community could be a foretaste of the New World Order on a smaller scale. The twelve European nations involved are seeking, among other things, a common economy, foreign policy, defense policy, and a common currency by 1999.

The New Age movement is like a puzzle or mosaic, but we can begin to see now how all the pieces could be fitting together. We can recognize that many of the seemingly unrelated, disconnected practices and teachings of the New Age movement affecting us today are leading to the ultimate goal of a one-world order. All of us in one way or another have been touched by the influence of the New Age movement and will continue to be affected by it as the plan for a New World Order unfolds. The task of achieving this one-world order will require more than human effort and wisdom. It will necessitate reprogramming and controlling the minds of every inhabitant of this planet, of every person in a single generation. And this is exactly what Satan, through the New Age, has been attempting to do by way of the subtle means discussed in this book!

• More and more New Age programming is being fed to TV viewers, portraying these concepts as the accepted norm and replacing Christian morals and values.

• Occult TV cartoons, toys, and electronic games are conditioning our children's minds to accept New Age occult practices and philosophies, choking off their Christian heritage.

• Thousands of Christians are being led into occult practices through the doorway of holistic medicine and parapsychology.

• Business seminars teaching Positive Mental Attitude and Christian seminars promoting Possibility Thinking are subtly replacing genuine faith and reliance on God with self-centered philosophies. Self and its improvement are becoming the all-absorbing themes of this generation.

• New Age stores are becoming increasingly popular as they offer ecological items and natural themes, conditioning people to the concept of a secular global and ecological consciousness in preparation for religious and governmental unification in the New World Order.

• The New Age teaching that there is divinity within each of us and that we are all divinely united becomes a key reason for global unity.

• Bookstores carry "Christian" books that contain occult and pagan theories disguised as "new" knowledge, thereby confusing and corrupting Christian morals and concepts through these subtle assaults on the mind.

• Education is conditioning children to view the world, not as many countries, but as one global community. Through the use of visualization and guided imagery, "spirit guides" are introduced, and children are encouraged to accept their advice without question.

• Movies perhaps play one of the most effective roles in promoting New Age beliefs and philosophies. While being entertained, seeds of error are sown into the fertile mind that, in short time, take hold and flourish.

• In the area of metaphysics and parapsychology, the fad of "going within" through various methods or techniques of meditation not only leads people to believe that the answers to life's problems lie within themselves, but also in many cases opens up the way to communication with supernatural, evil spirits.

• As a blend of Eastern and Western religions, the New Age movement is a perfect vehicle for a global, generic religion in which Catholics, Protestants, and others will unite under the New World Order.

When human minds have become heavily influenced or guided by the New Age movement, it will be no problem for Satan to step in and assume the controls that have already been put in place. The spiritual implications are tremendously disturbing.

If Western countries are going to initiate globalism, they need to set the precedent for a new unitive generic religion, since religion itself is an enormous factor in creating lines of demarcation and thus preventing transnational unity from happening. Therefore, a new type of spirituality is needed: one that disavows the old order, one that can synthesize the beliefs of both East and West. . . . But there is a movement afoot that attracts increasing numbers of educated, globally minded people in the West. . . . It is the New Age movement. This has enormous implications for the direction and even the survival of religious freedoms.[29]

Christians have known from the inspiration of the Bible that in the last days there would be an attempt at some kind of world domination. Revelation 13 tells of a power that will cause all who refuse to receive its mark to suffer economic and religious persecution, being unable to buy or sell.

God's New World Order

But God has also shown us in His word the end of this world's story. When men are experimenting with their New World Order, God will intervene. Daniel 2 speaks of a stone made without hands that will smite the feet of a metallic image representing the governments of this world. Paul tells us that just before the second coming of Christ, Satan, the imposter, will transform himself into an angel of light, leading many to believe that he is the saviour of the world (see 2 Corinthians 11:14). Matthew 24 tells us of the real Christ coming with "power and great glory" (verse 30). All the signs prophesied in that chapter have been or are being fulfilled right before our eyes. It is my firm belief that Christ will come within the time of our own generation, that many who are reading these pages will be alive to see this magnificent event, the glorious hope of all Christians. It's time to look up!

Revelation 21 and 22 prophesy of the New Jerusalem, prepared by God for those who are faithful to Him.

> And I saw a new heaven and a new earth: for the first heaven and the first earth were passed away; and there was no more sea. And I John saw the holy city, new Jerusalem, coming down from God out of heaven, prepared as a bride adorned for her husband. And I heard a great voice out of heaven saying, Behold, the tabernacle of God is with men, and he will dwell with them, and they shall be his people, and God himself shall be with them, and be their God. And God shall wipe away all tears from their eyes; and there shall be no more death, neither sorrow, nor crying, neither shall there be any more pain: for the former things are passed away. And he that sat upon the throne said, Behold, I make all things new. And he said unto me, Write: for these words are true and faithful (Revelation 21:1-5).

This, my friend, is the real New World Order that will last forever. Those who become citizens of God's New World will never again be touched by the New Age movement, for its evil power and its instigator will have perished with the old world order. Amen!

1. "The Holy Alliance," *Time* magazine, 24 February 1992, 30.
2. "Holy Alliance," *Time* magazine, 24 February 1992, 31.
3. "Holy Alliance," *Time* magazine, 24 February 1992, 28, 29.
4. Charles Krauthammer, "The Lonely Superpower," *The New Republic*, 29 July 1991, 23.
5. Clifford Goldstein, *Liberty*, January/February 1992, 17.
6. Kenneth L. Woodward with Frank Gibney, Jr., "Public Enemy Number One," *Newsweek*, 26 August 1991, 47.
7. Malachi Martin, *The Keys of This Blood* (New York: Simon and Schuster, 1990), 374.
8. Ibid., 15.
9. Ibid.
10. Ibid., 15, 16.
11. Ibid., 375.
12. Ibid., 639.
13. Ibid., 19.
14. "Washington Whispers," *U.S. News & World Report*, 13 August 1990, 18.
15. Charles Krauthammer, "The Lonely Superpower," *The New Republic*, 29 July 1991, 23.
16. *Los Angeles Times*, 14 April 1991.
17. *Newsweek*, 12 August 1991, 33.
18. *Christian Coalition Road to Victory II Conference and Strategy Briefing*, report by Dr. G. Edward Reid, Esq., 1.
19. Ibid., 11.
20. Ibid., 5.
21. Ibid., 8, 9.
22. Marilyn Ferguson, *The Aquarian Conspiracy* (Los Angeles: J. P. Tarcher, Inc. 1987), 405.
23. Ibid., 407.
24. Eric Buehrer, *The New Age Masquerade* (Brentwood, Tenn.: Wolgemuth & Hyatt Publishers, Inc., 1990), 115.
25. Al Gore, *Earth in the Balance* (Boston: Houghton Mifflin Co., 1992), 297.
26. Dave Hunt, *Global Peace and the Rise of Antichrist* (Eugene, Oreg.: Harvest House Publishers, 1990), 165, 166.
27. Mario Veloso, "Earth Summit—A Report," unpublished report, 9.
28. Tal Brooke, *When the World Will Be As One* (Eugene, Oreg.: Harvest House, 1989), 58.
29. Ibid., 203.

Epilogue

Now that you have finished reading the book, there should be little question in your mind that the tentacles of the subtle New Age movement have penetrated virtually all areas of society. It has even invaded the very privacy of our own homes. You know that the New Age is not compatible with Christianity and could even make inroads into your religious beliefs. So, what should you do about it?

First, there are some things that you should *not* do:

1. Now that you are more aware of some of the specific dangers of the New Age, one of the worst things you could do would be to begin to scrutinize, criticize, and ostracize those Christians you know who may be into some phase of the New Age. Many are unwittingly embracing these dangerously misleading concepts. Instead of being singled out or ostracized, they need to be warned in a loving way. You may find a Christian doctor in your church who is practicing acupuncture. He may be unaware that it is one of the entry points into the New Age. Speak to him privately, in a genuinely concerned way. You may notice that the background music being played in your church is New Age. Find out who's in charge of the music and speak privately to that person about possibly replacing it with another type of music. Your pastor may be into meditation and perhaps even teaching it to his congregation. Again, speak to him personally.

The last thing we need as Christians is to become fragmented. The New Age is anti-Christian, and if we fall into the trap of criticizing and ostracizing each other, it would serve the purpose of the New Age movement as well as anything we could do.

Christians need to be united. If we see error, we should follow the counsel of Christ in Matthew 7. Mention it privately to the person involved.

2. Do not become too intrigued with New Age teachings and practices. While you may wish to become more acquainted with the extent of New Age influence and ways of combating it, I would not recommend delving into the hard-core books on its teachings just out of curiosity. Truth lies so close to error in many of these areas that it could be spiritually dangerous to probe too deeply. Besides, many New Age books are inspired by spirit entities and as such should be avoided by Christians. There are many excellent books written by Christian authors warning about the New Age; you can become more knowledgeable on the subject through these. While it is not an exhaustive list, I have mentioned some of those books in the "Further Study" section beginning on page 139.

Some of the positive steps you can take are:

1. Begin cleaning house, both literally and figuratively. Remove whatever New Age influences you may have discovered in your own life. It may be movies or TV programs, New Age health or meditational practices, horoscopes or dabbling into the occult. Ask God to help you resolve to give up whatever habits or practices Satan is trying to deceive you with.

2. If you have children, begin to alert them to the dangers of their TV programs, toys, electronic games, reading materials, and any other areas you feel are adversely affecting their spiritual growth. With older children, you may encounter some resistance or reluctance to give up the harmful entertainment. Take time to discuss the situation and express your sincere concern for their spiritual well-being.

One of the arguments young people give is that TV programs, electronic games, reading, etc., does not affect them. They see no visible change or immediate consequence of their entertainment. Take time to show them that what they are taking into their minds could very well lie dormant for a period of time with no apparent outward affect. But when the right circumstances occur, this stored-up information can cause a chain of thought that could lead to disastrous results.

3. Begin to root and ground yourself in biblical Christian beliefs. Be so firmly committed to Christ and His teachings that you will be

able to stand for the right though the heavens fall. Be sure you understand the biblical teaching on the state of the dead, for this is at the core of New Age thinking and Satan's lie, "Thou shalt not surely die."

4. Pray for spiritual discernment, for tact and wisdom when witnessing to a New Ager. Remember, they are usually very "spiritual" in a different sense from Christians, but nevertheless spiritual. Don't try to argue away their philosophies or explain the major doctrines of the church. You should confront and overwhelm a New Ager with God's claims on his life and his need of Christ's saving grace. Share with him God's concern and unconditional love for him. This will blow his mind, especially if you do it with the conviction and authority of the Holy Spirit.

When Caryl Matrisciana was converted from the New Age movement to Christianity, it was through Richard, a young Christian, who asked her some very direct questions about her relationship to God and Christ, her Saviour. No one had ever approached her with Christianity quite this way before. All her beliefs in Lord Hari Krishna, Karma law, and spirit entities were no match for the beautifully simple plan of salvation. She diligently studied the passages that Richard wrote down for her and came under conviction. Today she is a Christian, crusading to help rescue other New Agers from Satan and win them back to Christ.

Appendix

Hebrew and Greek words translated in the Bible as "to meditate," or "meditation."

1. *Hagah.* "To meditate, mutter."
   Joshua 1:8 "Thou shalt meditate therein day and night."
   Psalm 1:2 "In his law doth he meditate day and night."
   Psalm 63:6 "When I . . . meditate on thee in the night watches."
   Psalm 77:12 "I will meditate also of all thy work."
   Psalm 143:5 "I meditate on all thy works."
   Isaiah 33:18 "Thine heart shall meditate terror."

2. *Siach, suach.* "To bow down, muse, meditate."
   Genesis 24:63 "Isaac went out to meditate in the field."
   Psalm 119:15 "I will meditate in thy precepts."
   Psalm 119:23 "Thy servant did meditate in thy statutes."
   Psalm 119:48 "I will meditate in thy statutes."
   Psalm 119:78 "I will meditate in thy precepts."
   Psalm 119:148 "That I might meditate in thy word."

3. *Meletao, promeletao.* "To be careful, take care."
   1 Timothy 4:15 "Meditate upon these things."
   Luke 21:14 "Settle it . . . not to meditate before what ye shall answer."

4. *Haguth.* "Meditation."
   Psalm 49:3 "The meditation of my heart shall be of understanding."

5. *Hagig.* "Earnest meditation."
   Psalm 5:1 "O Lord, consider my meditation."

6. *Higgayon.* "Meditation."
   Psalm 19:14 "Let . . . the meditation of my heart, be acceptable."

7. *Siach.* "Meditation."
   Psalm 104:34 "My meditation of him shall be sweet."

8. *Sichah.* "A bowing down, musing."
   Psalm 119:97 "It [thy law] is my meditation all the day."
   Psalm 119:99 "Thy testimonies are my meditation."

Glossary

Acupuncture / acupressure

Holistic health techniques that attempt to unblock and balance cosmic energy flow through inserting needles (acupuncture) or using pressure (acupressure) at key points on the body. Based on the Chinese Taoist yin-and-yang philosophy (the harmonious union of opposites).

Altered states

States of mind other than the normal consciousness; includes trance, hypnosis, mystical meditation, drug-induced states, and spirit possession.

Anchoring

A neurolinguistic process that hypnotically plants messages into the subconscious.

Astrology

The pseudoscience of interpreting the supposed influence of the celestial bodies and cosmic forces on human affairs and events. Based on the concept that the earth is at the center of the universe, encircled by the zodiac.

Aura

An atmosphere or luminous radiation surrounding a body or any other animate object. This envelope, or electric field, is described as having color, which indicates the person's physical, psychological, and spiritual condition.

Biofeedback

The technique of bringing bodily processes that are normally involuntary (heartbeat, breathing, brain waves, muscle tension, etc.) under conscious mental control. Through meditation, or yoga, a patient can learn to control what is normally involuntary.

Black magic

Magic that is negative and harmful, such as casting spells and curses; usually employed by witches, demons, and wizards. The opposite of white magic.

Centering

Another name for guided imagery, focusing, or visualization. Focusing on an object or mental image to induce meditation.

Channeling

Becoming a conduit for receiving and relaying messages or information from an unseen, departed spirit or a universal entity. The modern equivalent of the same practice performed by spiritualist mediums.

Chakras

The seven supposed energy points on the body, according to Eastern religions and New Agers. These chakras all supposedly have different colors and relate to the different organs and functions of the body.

Charm

An object worn to ward off evil or bring good fortune.

Clairvoyance

The ability to mentally see physical objects or events taking place beyond the view of physical sight.

Consciousness

The normal state of conscious life. Awareness of one's present and physical state and surroundings.

Coven
A group of satanists or witches (not to exceed thirteen in number) who come together for worship.

Crystals
Semiprecious stones such as quartz crystal, amethyst, and tourmaline, that are believed to possess healing properties.

Cult
A religious group in which the authority of its spiritual founder is regarded as equal to or greater than the Holy Scriptures.

Curse
A spell invoked against a person.

Divination
Receiving information concerning a person or object through supernatural revelation.

Ecology
The relationships between organisms and their environments.

ESP
Extrasensory perception. The psychic ability to perceive an event or situation through some way other than through the ordinary or usual senses.

Eastern religions
Hinduism, Buddhism, Zen Buddhism, and Taoism.

Familiar
A spirit embodied in an animal who serves or guards a person.

Gnosticism
The belief that through knowledge of secret doctrines and practices a person is enlightened and emancipated.

Guided imagery
Suggestions of one person to guide another person in the act of imagining or visualizing during meditation.

Guru
   A spiritual teacher or master who teaches the way of "enlightenment" to his followers.

Hatha yoga
   An Eastern religious spiritual discipline, taught in the Western
   hemisphere as a meditative exercise.

Herbalism
   Treatment of disease based on the use of medicinal plants. Some
   believe that each plant has a "spirit" with which they can
   communicate.

Higher self
   The superconsciousness or "god within."

Holistic
   Concerned with the whole: body, mind, and spirit.

Homeopathy
   Treatment of disease with small doses of otherwise harmful
   medicine based on the belief that "like cures like."

Horoscope
   A diagram of planet positions and zodiac signs at a specific time.
   Used by astrologers in suggesting character traits and foretell-
   ing events in an individual's life.

Hypnosis
   An altered state of consciousness or trance in which the individual is vulnerable to suggestions.

Humanism
   A philosophy that rejects supernaturalism and stresses an
   individual's worth and realization through reason.

I ching
   A Chinese book of divination containing the teachings of an ancient
   system of fortune telling in which sticks of different lengths are
   thrown and the resulting figures created are interpreted.

Incantation

The use of spells or of spoken or sung words in a mystical ritual. Sometimes used to induce meditation.

Invocation

A call for help. In spirit worship, the calling forth of demons.

Iridology

Use of the iris of the eye as a diagnostic tool for physical disorders based on the belief that the eye is the window of the body.

Karma

The belief that one's status in life is due to the good or bad things done in previous lives and that the karma of this present existence will determine what one will be in the next life.

Kinesiology

The science or study of human muscular movements. As used in New Age medicine, it involves diagnosis and treatment of disease through muscle testing based on a belief in universal cosmic energy and that man is an integral part of the universe.

Kundalini

A psycho-spiritual power believed to be lying dormant at the base of the spine where the root chakra is located.

Levitation

The supernatural raising of a person or thing with no physical support.

Lotus

A water lily thought to be sacred by Hindus and Buddhists. The opening of its petals are symbolic of the opening of the fourth or heart chakra to receive spirit or cosmic energies.

Macrobiotics

A low-fat diet and rigid lifestyle based on Taoist concepts. It involves a meditative altered state of consciousness while eating.

Magic
   Witchcraft, sorcery, or casting of spells to control events or govern certain natural or supernatural forces.

Magick
   Spelled with a "k" to distinguish it from magic as a charm or spell. This is a more systematic occult lifestyle such as outlined by Aleister Crowley, an authority who wrote many books on the subject.

Mantra
   A word or phrase chanted in preparation for meditation.

Massage therapy
   Using the hands to relieve strain or tension by manipulation of the muscles. In New Age medicine, a practice based on the concept of monism.

Meditation (New Age)
   Stilling the mind and senses so internal awareness becomes acute.

Monism
   An occult philosophy and basic New Age belief that "All is one." Monism makes no distinction between God and creation.

Mysticism
   The belief that communion with God is through subjective experience such as intuition or insight.

Necromancy
   Conjuring up spirits of the dead in order to reveal the future or influence events.

Neopagan
   New paganism.

Neurolinguistics
   Observing and interpreting body language to aid a counselor in helping his client overcome negative or undesirable behavior.

New Age movement
A spiritual, social, and political movement whose goal is to change individuals through mystical enlightenment in preparation for the entrance of a new age or new world order.

New World Order
Plan for a one-world government.

Nirvana
Final state of oblivion that Buddhists seek through extinction of desire and individual consciousness.

Numerology
The study of the occult significance of numbers.

Occult
Secret knowledge or supernatural powers. Mysterious, concealed matters.

Omen
A sign or phenomenon believed to be prophetic.

Ouija board
A game board with letters and numbers used to communicate with spirits.

Out-of-body experience
A mystical experience in which the body remains in place while the mind travels through other planes of consciousness.

Pantheism
A belief that equates God with the forces and laws of the universe. Therefore He is impersonal and present in everything.

Paradigm shift
A major turn in the way of thinking.

Paranormal
Outside the normally understood process of cause and effect.

Parapsychology
The study of paranormal psychological phenomena (telepathy, clairvoyance, etc.).

Pentagram
A five-pointed star. With two points up, it represents Satan.

Possibility Thinking / Positive Mental Attitude
The concept that "whatever your mind can conceive, it can achieve." This idea is based on the belief that the human mind has inherent powers that are capable of creating one's own reality.

Psi
A New Age term for such paranormal phenomena as ESP, clairvoyance, telepathy, etc.

Psychic
A medium or channeler.

Psychokinesis
Ability to move physical objects solely through the powers of the mind.

Reflexology
An energy manipulating therapy using massage or pressure on certain areas of the feet to cause change in other parts of the body.

Reincarnation
Also called "rebirthing." The teaching that the soul is eternal and exists in a continuous life cycle until it reaches "nirvana," a state of nothingness. Good or bad actions in one life affect the condition of the next.

Shamanism
A system of healing through a person who enters into altered consciousness to communicate with the spirit world.

Spirit guide
A conjured-up entity who gives advice to humans.

Sorcery
Use of magic to alter events, for good or evil.

Tantra
Hindu and Buddhist scriptures dealing with techniques and rituals of meditative and sexual practices.

Tao
Chinese concept of the path of virtuous conduct. Obtaining long life and good fortune by magical means.

Talisman
A charm worn to gain supernatural protection or good luck.

Tarot
Cards used for fortune telling.

Telepathy
Communication between minds by extrasensory means.

Theosophy
Teaching of God and the world based on mystery religions and Hindu philosophies.

Therapeutic touch
An energy-manipulating therapy that seeks to unblock energy in order to restore health.

Third eye
Occult belief that in the center of the forehead there exists a spiritually intuitive center of consciousness. In yoga it's called the seventh chakra of enlightenment.

Trance
A state of deep hypnosis.

Transcendental
Religious means of reaching higher consciousness through the practice of meditation.

Triangle
   Used as a symbol of Satan.

Universal energy
   An unseen force in the universe believed to be God. Can be controlled for good or bad.

Unicorn
   A mythical animal with body and head of horse, hind legs of a stag, tail of a lion, and a horn in the middle of the forehead.

Unisex (androgyny)
   Belief that humans are composed of equal male and female sides. Each sex needs to get in touch with his/her other side.

Vedas
   The oldest Hindu scriptures.

Visualization
   An attempt to create reality through the imagination during altered states of consciousness.

Warlock
   A male witch.

White magic
   Supposedly helpful or beneficial supernatural power. Opposed to black magic.

Wicca
   An assembly or band of thirteen witches.

Witchcraft
   The practice of sorcery or mystical powers.

Yin/Yang
   Ancient Chinese symbol for the theory of the unity of opposites.

Yoga
   A Hindu discipline teaching suppression of all bodily and mental activity in an attempt to liberate oneself from reality.

Yogi

One who practices and teaches the methods of yoga.

Zen

A type of Buddhist thought that aims at enlightenment by direct intuition through meditation.

Zodiac

An imaginary belt in the heavens encompassing the apparent paths of the planets; used for predictions in astrology.

For
Further Study

General view of the New Age movement:
Wade, Kenneth R., *Secrets of the New Age.* Hagerstown, Md.: Review and Herald Publishing Association, 1989.

Chandler, Russell, *Understanding the New Age.* Dallas: Word Publishing, 1991.

Hoyt, Karen, *The New Age Rage*, Old Tappan, N.J.: Fleming H. Revell Company, 1978.

Hunt, Dave, and McMahon, T. A., *The Seduction of Christianity, Spiritual Discernment in the Last Days.* Eugene, Oreg.: Harvest House Publishers, 1987.

Personal testimonies by those coming out of New Age:
Baron, Will, *Deceived by the New Age.* Boise, Idaho: Pacific Press, 1990.

Matrisciana, Caryl, *Gods of the New Age.* Eugene, Oreg.: Harvest House Publishers, 1985.

Holistic health:
Peters, Warren, *Mystical Medicine.* Rapidan, Va.: Hartland Publications, 1987.

Sneed, David, and Sneed, Sharon, *The Hidden Agenda: A Critical View of Alternative Medical Therapies*. Nashville: Thomas Nelson Publishers, 1991.

Ankerberg, John, and Weldon, John, *The Facts on Holistic Health and the New Medicine*. Eugene, Oreg.: Harvest House Publishers, 1992.

New Age and occult symbols:
Steed, Ernest, *Two Be One*. Plainfield, N.J.: Logos International, 1978.

Marrs, Texe, *Dark Secrets of the New Age*. Westchester, Ill.: Crossway Books, 1987.

Occult TV cartoons and toys:
Robie, Joan Hake, *Turmoil in the Toybox II*. Lancaster, Pa.: Starburst Publishers, 1989.

Phillips, Phil, *Saturday Morning Mind Control*. Nashville, Tenn.: Thomas Nelson Publishers, 1991.

New World Order:
Brooke, Tal, *When the World Will Be As One*. Eugene, Oreg.: Harvest House, 1989.

New Age in Education:
Buehrer, Eric, *The New Age Masquerade*. Brentwood, Tenn.: Wolgemuth & Hyatt Publishers, Inc., 1990.

Biblical meditation/New Age meditation:
Goldberg, Keith A., *How to Respond to Transcendental Meditation*. St. Louis: Concordia, 1977.

Horoscopes:
Morey, Robert A., *Horoscopes and the Christian*. Minneapolis, Minn.: Bethany House Publishers, 1981.

Bibliography

Ankerberg, John, and Weldon, John, *The Facts on False Teaching in the Church*. Eugene, Oreg.: Harvest House, 1988.

_____. *The Facts on Holistic Health and the New Medicine*. Eugene, Oreg.: Harvest House, 1992.

_____. *The Facts on the New Age Movement*. Eugene, Oreg.: Harvest House, 1988.

Bach, Richard, *Jonathan Livingston Seagull*. New York: Avon Publishers, 1970.

Baron, Will, *Deceived by the New Age*. Boise, Idaho: Pacific Press, 1990.

Bayley, Doreen E., *Reflexology Today*. Rochester, Vt.: Healing Arts Press, 1988.

Buehrer, Eric, *The New Age Masquerade*. Brentwood, Tenn.: Wolgemuth & Hyatt Publishers, Inc., 1990.

Chandler, Russell, *Understanding the New Age*. Dallas: Word Publishing, 1988.

Cumbey, Constance, *The Hidden Dangers of the Rainbow*. Lafayette, La.: Huntington House, Inc., 1983.

DeMoss, Robert G., Jr., *Learn to Discern*. Grand Rapids: Zondervan Publishing House, 1992.

Dragon Warrior Strategy Guide. Nintendo of America, Inc., and Tokuma Shoten, 1989.

Ferguson, Marilyn, *The Aquarian Conspiracy*. Los Angeles: J. P. Tarcher, Inc., 1987.

Foster, Richard J., *Celebration of Discipline*. San Francisco: Harper and Row, 1988.

Froom, LeRoy Edwin, *Spiritualism Today*. Washington, D.C.: Review and Herald Publishing Association, 1963.

Gawain, Shakti, *Creative Visualization*. New York: Bantam Books, 1982.

Gerberding, Keith A., *How to Respond to Transcendental Meditation*. St. Louis: Concordia, 1977.

Ghostbusters II. Film by Columbia Pictures Industries, Inc., 1989.

Gildstein, Joan, and Soares, Manuela, *The Joy Within*. New York: Prentice Hall, 1990.

Groothuis, Douglas, *Confronting the New Age*. Downers Grove, Ill.: InterVarsity Press, 1978.

Gorbachev, Mikhail, *Perestroika—New Thinking for Our Country and the World*. New York: Harper and Row, 1987.

Gore, Tipper, *Raising PG Kids in an X-Rated Society*. Nashville: Abingdon Press, 1987.

Hiller, B. B., *Teenage Mutant Ninja Turtles*. New York: Dell, 1990.

Hoyt, Karen, *The New Age Rage*. Old Tappan, N.J.: Fleming H. Revell Company, 1978.

Hunt, Dave, *Global Peace*. Eugene, Oreg.: Harvest House, 1990.

Hunt, Dave, and McMahon, T. A., *The Seduction of Christianity, Spiritual Discernment in the Last Days*. Eugene, Oreg.: Harvest House, 1987.

Hunt, Dave, *Understanding the New Age Movement*. Eugene, Oreg.: Harvest House, 1977.

Knight, J. Z., *A State of Mind, My Story*. New York: Warner Books, 1987.

Larson, Bob, *Straight Answers on the New Age*. Nashville: Thomas Nelson, 1989.

Leithart, Peter, and Grant, George, *A Christian Response to Dungeons and Dragons*. Fort Worth, Tex.: Dominion Press, 1987.

MacLaine, Shirley, *Going Within*. New York: Bantam Books, 1989.

_____. *Out on a Limb*. New York: Bantam Books, 1983.

Macrae, Janet, *Therapeutic Touch, A Practical Guide*. New York: Alfred A. Knopf, Inc., 1991.

Marrs, Texe, *Dark Secrets of the New Age*. Westchester, Ill.: Crossway Books, 1987.

_____. *Mystery Mark of the New Age*. Westchester, Ill.: Crossway Books, 1988.

_____. *Ravaged by the New Age*. Austin, Tex.: Living Truth Publishers, 1989.

Martin, Malachi, *The Keys of This Blood*. New York: Simon and Schuster, 1990.

Matrisciana, Caryl, *Gods of the New Age*. Eugene, Oreg.: Harvest House, 1985.

McMillen, S. I., *None of These Diseases*. Westwood, N.J.: Pyramid Publications, Inc., 1963.

Menconi, Al, *Today's Music: A Window to Your Child's Soul*. Elgin, Ill.: David C. Cook, 1990.

Michaelsen, Johanna, *Like Lambs to the Slaughter*. Eugene, Oreg.: Harvest House, 1989.

_____. *The Beautiful Side of Evil*. Eugene, Oreg.: Harvest House, 1982.

Milicevic, Barbara, *Your Spiritual Child, Primer for Metaphysics and Yoga*. Marina del Rey, Calif.: DeVorss and Co., 1984.

Morey, Robert A., *Horoscopes and the Christian*. Minneapolis, Minn.: Bethany House, 1981.

New Brown, Driver, and Briggs Hebrew and English Lexicon of the Old Testament. Grand Rapids: Baker Book House, n.d.

Noss, John B., *Man's Religions*. New York: Macmillan, 1974.

Novak, John (Joytish), *How to Meditate*. Crystal Clarity Publishers, 1989.

O'Brien, Justin, *Christianity and Yoga*. London: Arkana, 1989.

Peck, M. Scott, *The Road Less Traveled*. New York: Simon and Schuster, 1978.

Peters, Warren, *Mystical Medicine*. Rapidan, Va.: Hartland Publications, n.d.

Phillips, Phil, *Saturday Morning Mind Control*. Nashville, Tenn.: Thomas Nelson, 1991.

Robie, Joan Hake, *Turmoil in the Toybox II*. Lancaster, Pa.: Starburst Publishers, 1989.

Rosten, Leo, *A Guide to the Religions of America*. New York: Simon and Schuster, 1955.

Shealy, C. Norman, M.D., with Freese, Arthur S., *Occult Medicine Can Save Your Life*. Columbus, Ohio: The Dial Press, 1975.

Short, Robert, *The Gospel From Outer Space*. New York: Harper and Row, 1983.

Smith, Huston, *The Religions of Man*. New York: NAL, 1958.

Sneed, David, and Sneed, Sharon, *The Hidden Agenda*. Nashville: Thomas Nelson, 1991.

Snelling, John, *The Buddhist Handbook*. Rochester, Vt.: Inner Traditions, 1991.

Tao Te Ching, translation by R. B. Blakney, *The Way of Life Lao Tzu*. New York: Mentor Books, 1983.

Sutton, William Josiah, *The New Age Movement and The Illuminati 666*. The Institute of Religious Knowledge, 1983.

Wade, Kenneth R., *Secrets of the New Age*. Hagerstown, Md.: Review and Herald Publishing Association, 1989.

Wade, T. E., *Spirit Possession*. Auburn, Calif.: Gazelle Publications, 1991.

White, Ellen G., *Evangelism*. Washington, D.C.: Review and Herald Publishing Association, 1946.

White, Ellen G., *Steps to Christ*. Mountain View, Calif.: Pacific Press Publishing Association, 1956.

WE STILL BELIEVE

by Robert Folkenberg

A century and a half after the 1844 disappointment, can we seriously say that Jesus is coming "soon"? The leader of the worldwide Seventh-day Adventist Church boldly proclaims that **"WE STILL BELIEVE."**

Elder Folkenberg honestly looks at the challenges and questions that the delay poses and assures us that we can, indeed, have unshakable confidence that Jesus is coming soon and the early advent teachings are still relevant.

At a time when doubt and cyncism threaten our advent hope, this faith-restoring book will help you affirm the truth that *we still believe*!

US$8.95/Cdn$13.00. Paper.